SUCCESSFUL SELLING TIPS
for INTROVERTED AUTHORS

SUCCESSFUL SELLING TIPS

for INTROVERTED AUTHORS

**YES!
WE CAN!**

Kim Staflund

Calgary Herald Bestselling Author

Successful Selling Tips for Introverted Authors

With special thanks to the following valued contributors to this book:
Susan Chambers, Copy editing and fact checking
Ted Ruybal, Graphic design of cover and interior
Tia Leschke, Indexing
Pamela Sourelis, Proofreading
Melissa Leech and Kim Staflund, Additional proofreading

Added thanks to all who helped with the author photo:
Paige Gesell of Life Photo Studios, Photography
Zoey Williams of Lavish Salon, Make-up artistry
Heather Marshall of Lavish Salon, Hairstyling
Happy Choice Nail & Spa, Northland Mall, Manicure

Additional copies of this book may be ordered by visiting the
PPG Online Bookstore at:

shop.polishedpublishinggroup.com

Due to the dynamic nature of the Internet, any website addresses mentioned within this book might have been changed or discontinued since its publication. Any resemblance between the sample books listed herein and anyone else's actual book is purely coincidental.
All the royalty calculations for these sample books are hypothetical.

"INTROVERTS UNITE! (. . . AT HOME . . . ONLINE)"

~Author unknown

FOR INTROVERTED AUTHORS
THE WORLD OVER.

TABLE OF CONTENTS

FIRST THINGS FIRST: LET'S CONQUER OUR FEARS

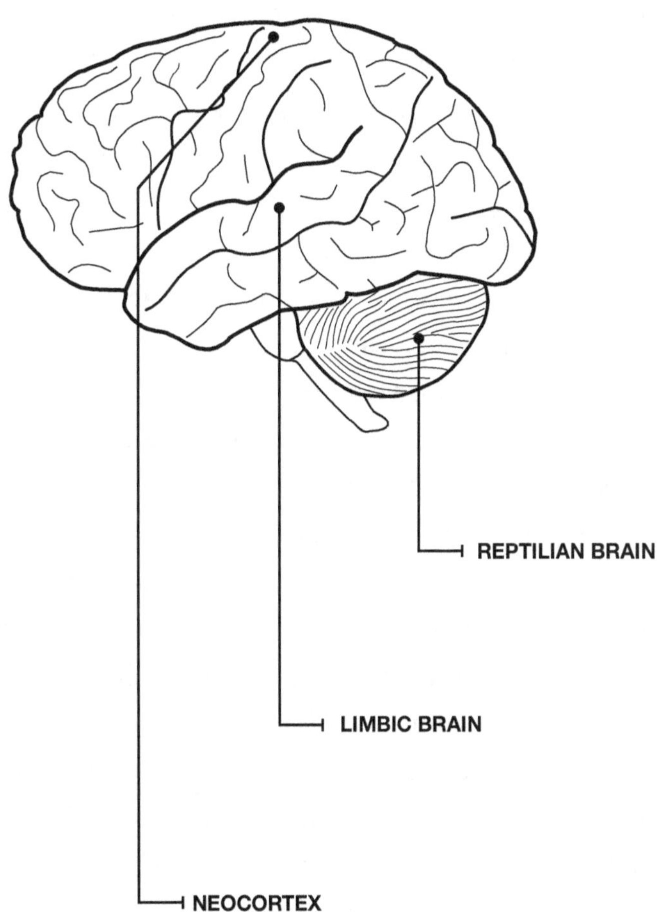

Very early into my career as a book publisher, I decided to offer opportunities for authors to publish their books free of charge with my company, Polished Publishing Group (PPG). I did this because of my naïve assumption that there was only one thing standing in the way of people choosing my company as their book publisher over some of my competitors—price. The majority of my competitors either used the low-cost vanity book publishing business model to produce books for indie authors, or they were traditional trade publishers who charged authors nothing at all in exchange for copyright ownership of the book. By contrast, I ran my company using a hybrid business model, known as supported self-publishing, that ensured the polished, professional result you get with a trade publisher along with the maintained copyright ownership you get with a vanity publisher. Professional quality costs more.

I wanted to be competitive in the marketplace. But even more than that, I wanted to ensure that all authors had access to *professional*-quality book publishing—even those who couldn't easily afford the full cost. So, I offered this opportunity to them in the form of contests.

The first year, I took out a specialty insurance policy which allowed PPG to offer authors a chance to win $100,000 in cash if they referred aspiring authors to us who ended up purchasing one of our book publishing packages, if they purchased one of our book publishing packages toward the publication of their own book, or if they could prove they sold fifty copies of their already-published PPG book in a bookstore consignment deal. Long story short, there were very few entries into this contest and nobody won. I deemed this experiment unsuccessful because it didn't drum up anywhere near the new business I had hoped for; and, I attributed that lack of interest to the fact that it required people to invest a significant amount of time or money upfront for a chance to win, and that it was only a chance instead of a guarantee that at least one person would win.

So the next year, I offered a chance to win $5,000 toward a professional PPG publishing package to all Canadian adults aged eighteen years or older with a guarantee that one person would win. This time, no one had to pay any money upfront. People could qualify for more than one chance to win in various ways: by liking our Facebook page; by following us on Twitter; by subscribing to the PPG Publisher's Blog; or by joining the PPG Writers Forum. I figured there would be much more interest across the country—and there *was*—but something curious happened. Despite the fact that we had quite a few contestants and one seemingly solid winner, a book was never published as a result of this contest.

Despite being given the opportunity—the written *guarantee!*—to have a professional-quality book published free of charge, in which 100 percent copyright ownership of both the written words and the artwork produced for that project would remain with the author, our winner still procrastinated on publishing the book for several months. Halfway through the year, we had a conversation about this. I expressed to this author that the prize was to have a book published *within* the year; and if we didn't begin the publication process within the next month or two, it would be impossible to have it completed within the year, which would render the contest null and void. I provided a deadline that the winner agreed to meet; and it was also agreed that if we didn't begin publication of the book by that date then, out of fairness to the other contestants, the contest would be re-opened to them.

The winner procrastinated some more . . . right past the agreed-upon deadline. So, a letter was sent out to all of the contestants (including the winner) offering everyone one more crack at this prize. This letter was also posted publicly on the PPG Facebook Page (Polished Publishing Group, 2015a). Due to the lateness in the year, everyone was given two weeks to submit their properly-formatted manuscripts (including all front matter, body, back matter, and back cover copy) and artwork to PPG in order to qualify, otherwise the contest would be deemed null and void. Four of these contestants (including the first winner) expressed a solid interest and said they had books ready to go, so it was hopeful for one gleaming moment in time that we might have ourselves a winner. But guess what happened? *Everyone* procrastinated past the deadline. No one submitted their work. The contest was deemed null and void.

I can vividly recall one of these contestants using the excuse of limited time. "It's going to take me four hours to put together everything you need in order to submit my book to you. I don't have that kind of time right now." I'll admit I was not only shocked by this but also a little annoyed. I didn't respond to the comment. I didn't know *how* to respond to that, because I found it so perplexing that someone would abandon $5,000 in free cash for only four hours of work. It was the equivalent of me paying that person *$1,250 per hour* to do what needed be done to get that book ready for our professional publishing process; and yet, this contestant *still* wouldn't (couldn't?) do it: nor would any of the others.

I've come to realize that an author's procrastination has very little to do with him or her being too frugal to invest the amount of money that is necessary to produce a professional quality book; because, even when given the opportunity to do it for free, many people still can't bring themselves to do it. And it has even *less* to do with simple laziness. This is about *fear*. Only an intense fear of something can prevent an author from publishing and selling his or her book. But a fear of *what*? That's the question.

Or maybe a more accurate way to word that question would be, "What exactly causes fear?" And perhaps the answer is simple genetics—a surplus, irrational "fight or flight" survival instinct that is still present in the human brain even after thousands of years of evolution. According to the website *The Brain from Top to Bottom*, written by Bruno Dubuc (2015) at McGill University,

The first time you observe the anatomy of the human brain, its many folds and overlapping structures can seem very confusing, and you may wonder what they all mean. But just like the anatomy of any other organ or organism, the anatomy of the brain becomes much clearer and more meaningful when you examine it in light of the evolutionary processes that created it.

Dubuc (2015) goes on to compare the three components of the human brain: the reptilian brain; the limbic brain; and the neocortex. Of these three components,

> The reptilian brain, the oldest of the three, controls the body's vital functions such as heart rate, breathing, body temperature and balance. Our reptilian brain includes the main structures found in a reptile's brain: the brainstem and the cerebellum. The reptilian brain is reliable but tends to be somewhat rigid and compulsive.

Your unconscious, compulsive, automatic fear of things unknown is created in the reptilian portion of your brain. It's purely instinctual, just like reptiles. They don't "think" or "rationalize" things through. Nor do they have any sort of emotional response to things. Reptiles simply react out of their natural survival instinct. When they are faced with a common situation that's known to them, they either live in/on it . . . or they eat it. When they are faced with a potentially threatening (unknown) situation, they run and hide. Theirs is a pretty simple, straightforward existence.

Instinct is a good thing that serves a valid purpose in our lives. God gave us all an instinct for a reason, and we should pay attention to it; but, whenever your fear of the unknown has you avoiding potentially advantageous opportunities simply because they're new to you, I encourage you to consult with your more evolutionarily advanced neocortex—the logical, rational portion of your brain—by writing your fears down. Articulate them to yourself in writing. Read them out loud to yourself. When you do this, you'll begin to see just how irrational many of those fears really are.

- ## Fear #1: What if it's a bad idea?

I can't tell you how many authors I've sat and had a coffee with who have sheepishly shrugged their shoulders and said, "It's probably a stupid idea. Maybe I shouldn't do it."

To which I always reply, "How long have you been thinking about this idea? When did it first come to you?"

For many of them, the answer is, "Several months." For others, the answer is, "Several years."

I always tell them the same thing: "An idea is a life form of its own that wishes to be expressed. It wants to be given life, and it has chosen *you* as the conduit for its life. That's a *gift*. Accept this gift and use your God-given talent to give it the expression and life it craves. The fact that you've been thinking about this idea for several months or years tells you that it's not simply a fleeting thought. It's a *real* living, breathing thing."

As an entrepreneur starting my own book publishing business, and writing and selling my own books, I had my moments when I thought to myself, "Maybe this is a bad idea." I'm just like you. What I did, in those moments, was seek out inspiration from other people who had succeeded before me, to help me push through that fear and self-doubt. I read books. I watched videos. I used whatever tools I could find to help myself move forward.

One of my most cherished sources of inspiration is a video of Sara Blakely (2011), the founder of Spanx, Inc., speaking to a group at The Edge Connection in Atlanta, Georgia, about how she built her hosiery company from a mere $5,000 initial investment into a billion dollar empire in a short ten years. Very early in her presentation, she describes listening to a speaker at a convention who stated that he would prove to the room, in only four words, that there is no such thing as a bad idea: TEENAGE MUTANT NINJA TURTLES! Sara herself eventually went on to prove to the many early doubters, in only two words, that there is no such thing as a bad idea: FOOTLESS PANTYHOSE!

I highly recommend this video of Sara Blakely to all authors who doubt themselves and their current ideas—whether it's a book topic idea or a sales idea you have for an already-published book. It is a beautiful example of what's possible when one pushes past that instinctive, reptilian-brain fear and perseveres in the achievement of a goal—any goal. For those who love humour, you'll enjoy this video all the more. This woman is not only inspirational; she's downright hilarious. I truly admire her on so many levels.

• Fear #2: What if nobody reads it?

Well, then nobody will read it. And you'll be no further behind nor any further ahead than you are today. You're surviving right now, right? Fear busted.

• Fear #3: What if people read it and don't like it?

First of all, if people are reading it, that's a good thing! That's the ultimate goal!

Second, accept the fact that you're entitled to your own opinions—and so is everyone else. Once you can do that, you'll experience a freedom you've never experienced before.

When I published my first book, everything was quite new to me, and I had an expectation (possibly an unfair one) that my friends and family members should support me 100 percent and compliment me on my book, no matter what they thought of it. Luckily, that did happen with my first book. Everyone around me was very supportive.

Unfortunately, when my second book came out, it was a different story. I received an unexpected criticism from someone dear to me that left me shocked, hurt, and unsure how to react. I'll be honest; it took me a couple years to come to a place where I was willing to put myself out there again. During that time, I had to rethink my expectations of those closest to me and find a way to remain confident in myself and my craft regardless of others' opinions.

In retrospect, I'm glad I experienced that criticism so early in my publishing career because it taught me a valuable lesson about how I should measure the true merit of my work. A few times, I've had to ask myself the question: What is the truth here? Is it the joy and enthusiasm I felt when I held a printed copy of the book in my hand for the very first time? Or is it the self-doubt I felt when someone criticized it later on? Which one of those two moments will I use to determine the value of my book?

A wise woman named Lisa Nichols once said in *The Secret* (Byrne, 2006)

> Oftentimes, you give others the opportunity to create your happiness, and many times they fail to create it the way you want it. Why? Because only one person can be in charge of your joy . . . and that's you. So even your parent, your child, your spouse—they do not have the control to create your happiness. They simply have the opportunity to share in your happiness. Your joy lies within you. (p. 122)

A beautiful sentiment, don't you think? I believe the same can be said for self-confidence and faith.

I've gone into every book project since then with a new set of expectations that take the pressure off both me and those around me. It's always nice when people acknowledge a new book with a hearty congratulation, but I've decided that's where their obligation ends. I no longer base a book's worth on whether others read it, agree with it, enjoy it, or discuss it with me after the fact. The truth I try my best to hold onto is the joy I felt when I held that first printed copy in my hand. I hope you will do the same for you. I hope you will find a way to hold onto your enthusiasm even if you come up against any criticism along the way—whether it's from friends, family members, reviewers, or anyone else. Keep writing! Keep the faith!

These are just some of the fears that come up *before* you've published your book, never mind the ones that creep in during the publishing process itself. And if that's not enough, once you get past those and actually publish your book, then there's the fear of book sales and marketing to contend with—the anxiety you feel at the idea of exposing yourself publicly. Julia Cameron (2002) put it best in her book titled *The Artist's Way* when she wrote:

> Do not call procrastination laziness. Call it fear. Fear is what blocks an artist. The fear of not being good enough. The fear of not finishing. The fear of failure and of success. The fear of beginning at all. There is only one cure for fear. The cure is love. Use love for your artist to cure its fear.

All of your concerns about book publishing, sales, and marketing are variations of the exact same thing: the reptilian brain's unconscious, automatic "fight or flight" survival instinct triggered by its fear of the unknown and coupled with its inability to feel love. And, perhaps, this instinct is so much more prevalent with introverted people than it is with extroverts because of our natural tendency to retreat from decidedly public situations, after short periods of time, if we're unfamiliar with the people in the room. It's common for us to withdraw even when no obvious threat is present. When it comes down to solitude versus unknown group settings, solitude is where we feel most comfortable, isn't it?

So, let's talk about it, from one introvert to another. Let's overcome these irrational fears together and learn how to work *with* our solitary nature instead of avoiding the very actions that could bring us success as authors.

My goal in writing this book is to do my best to put your reptilian mind at ease so you can use your neocortex more effectively in the successful sales and marketing of your book. In fact, you're going to use more than your logical neocortex. You're also going to learn how to put your emotional limbic brain to good use so you can appeal to others' limbic brains to get them to buy your book.

As Zig Ziglar, a well-known and often-quoted American author, salesman, and motivational speaker, so aptly stated, "People don't buy for logical reasons. They buy for emotional reasons" (cited in Kruse, 2012). The most effective salespeople appeal to their customers' *emotions* to sell their products and services. I hope to teach you some effective ways to do this that fit well with your introverted personality so you can sell more books and enjoy more success as an author. That is my intention.

AN INTRODUCTION TO SELLING FROM ONE INTROVERT TO ANOTHER

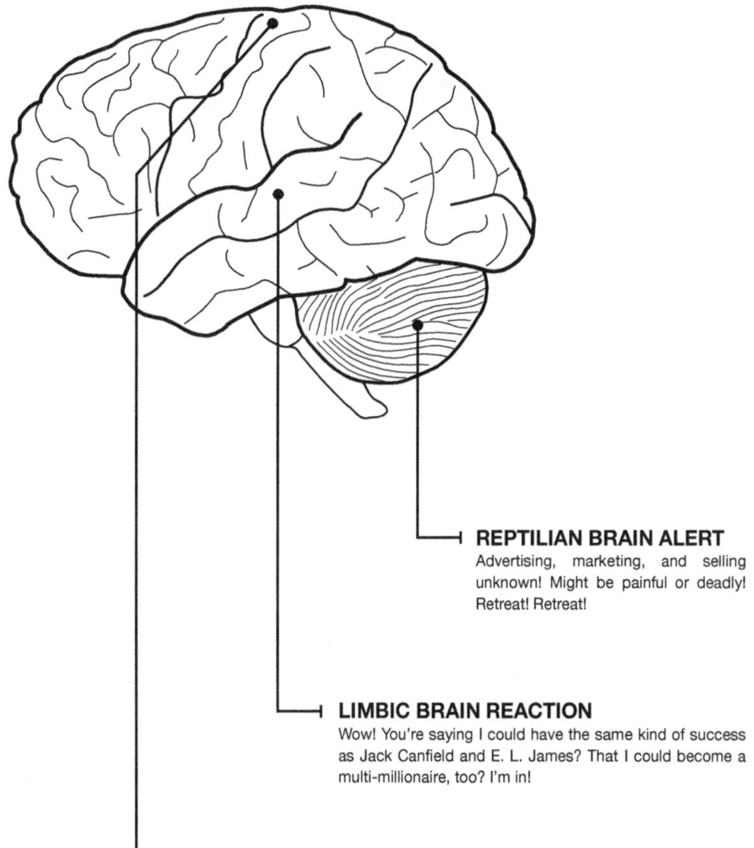

I've never been a natural salesperson, nor have I ever been naturally extroverted. These are learned skills that were, it seemed, forced upon me 20 years ago after working for a small literary publisher and learning, firsthand, the realities of the traditional trade book publishing industry. I'm a natural writer with introverted tendencies who takes great joy in spending countless hours in the solitude of my quiet office with nothing more than my laptop, my pen, my pad of paper, and my creative thoughts to keep me company. I've been a natural writer since I was old enough to write. But I've never been a natural salesperson.

As a natural writer, it was always my dream to become an author, but not just any old author. I wanted to become a *bestselling* author. And as an aspiring bestselling author, you can imagine how thrilled I was at age 21 when I started looking for work, one month shy of obtaining my college diploma in business management, and I came across a career ad in the daily newspaper for a job with a local literary book publisher. They needed someone for their accounts receivable and fulfillment area. With my new business management credentials, I had all the qualifications they required, so I applied. They called me for an interview a week or so later, and they hired me very soon after that. It was my in! I was thrilled by the opportunity to work for an established book publisher and learn the industry from the inside out. At the time, it was a dream come true for me because I was convinced that it would lead to the achievement of my life-long goal of becoming the published author of a bestselling book.

Now let me skip ahead three years and tell you this job was an eye-opening experience for someone like me with no prior concept of how book publishing, sales, and marketing all worked. Beforehand, I had romanticized about my future life as a "discovered" author whose only job was to spend time leisurely creating my next masterpiece, in whichever exotic locale I found most inspiring, while my publisher bustled about in the background, managing all the logistics—advertising, marketing, sales, and distribution—on my behalf. Of course, my books would be flying off the shelves with very little effort on my part, earning me millions of dollars in royalties in the process. My biggest concern would be somehow answering all those fan letters and selecting the perfect attire for each upcoming sold-out book signing event.

Back to reality . . .

Here's a rhetorical question for you: If it really was that simple and all it took to become a bestselling author was to publish a well-written book, wouldn't you already be a bestselling author?

Yes, there are the exceptions of the world—the J.K. Rowlings who strike gold without having to sell their books themselves. But the majority of us authors have to put some effort into it before we'll see any real profits. I'm pretty sure J.K. Rowling won't ever pick up a copy of this book because she doesn't have to, and I'm okay with that. I didn't write it for the exceptions—I wrote it for the majority.

It took me some time to come to terms with the realities of this industry for the majority of authors. It took me three years of working hard at that traditional literary press to figure out what worked and what didn't, to fully understand and appreciate the differences between our authors who saw success in their book sales versus the ones who didn't. At the end of those three years, I knew that was not the place where I was going to learn the skills I needed to become a bestselling author. I knew then that it would take more than simply my natural ability to write a great book.

Although I absolutely loved many aspects of my job—the books, my colleagues, our authors, organizing and attending all the book launch parties and signings each spring and fall—it was clear to me that there was little room for advancement and even less chance of a salary increase anytime soon. If I wanted to improve my personal situation and learn the skills to make my dream come true, it was more complicated than simply finding a new job within the publishing sector. I was going to have to find a new *industry* altogether. So, that's what I did: I found a job in advertising sales at the local daily newspaper and have worked in some type of sales capacity pretty much ever since.

Back then, it felt like defeat. I was disappointed to leave my first love, book publishing, and saw no possible way to return—unless I resigned myself to a life of low wages, which I refused to do! It also felt very foreign and uncomfortable for me to be in an advertising sales role. I *hated* sales back then! I resisted it, at first, which made it much more difficult than it had to be. It was as though the Fates were determined to keep me there, despite my resistance, and would only let me go once I fully embraced my role as a salesperson and became skilled enough at it to return to my first love in good form, which took me nearly two decades to accomplish. (I can be a bit stubborn when I feel held against my will.) In hindsight, the Fates were right all along. Moving into advertising sales turned out to be a brilliant stroke of luck. It taught me a most valuable skill set (not to mention *mindset)* that none of my colleagues from the traditional trade book publishing sector were ever able to teach me—and it would come in very handy later on.

Perhaps the most important lesson I learned over the years was the difference between advertising, marketing, and sales, and how they all work in conjunction with each other. Here are their definitions as per *The Free Dictionary* (2015a):

- **ad·ver·tis·ing (ăd'vər-tī'zǐng)**
  n.

  1. The activity of attracting public attention to a product or business, as by paid announcements in the print, broadcast, or electronic media.

  2. The business of designing and writing advertisements.

- ## mar·ket·ing (mär′kĭ-tĭng)

  n.

  1. The act or process of buying and selling in a market.

  2. The strategic functions involved in identifying and appealing to particular groups of consumers, often including activities such as advertising, branding, pricing, and sales.

- ## sell (sĕl)

  v. sold (sōld), sell·ing, sells

  v.tr.

  1. To exchange or deliver for money or its equivalent: *We sold our old car for a modest sum.*

  2. To offer or have available for sale: *The store sells health foods.*

  4. To be purchased in (a certain quantity); achieve sales of: *a book that sold a million copies.*

To clarify, advertising is the *vehicle* you use to reach your target market of customers. Marketing is the *language* in which you choose to speak to them to pique their interest in your offering. And selling is the *act* of convincing them to buy from you—of coming right out and asking for the sale. The most successful salespeople harmonize all three of these components together in a well thought-out sales campaign, which I intend to teach you how to do in this book.

Since leaving that literary press and learning these new skills, I have achieved my goal and become a bestselling author. To date, my books have been publicly listed as bestsellers on Amazon's Canadian, American, and United Kingdom ecommerce sites as well as in a traditional market—a prominent daily newspaper in one of Canada's major cities.

I've published six books in total (you are reading the sixth one right now), including my two most recent titles that compile all my knowledge of the book publishing industry, as a whole, into two compact and easy-to-read volumes: *How to Publish a Book in Canada . . . and Sell Enough Copies to Make a Profit!* (Staflund, 2013) and *How to Publish a Bestselling Book . . . and Sell It WORLDWIDE Based on Value, Not Price!* (Staflund, 2014). I highly recommend picking up a copy of either of these books to complement the lessons you will learn in this one because they contain answers to basically every question you've ever had about how to write, publish, copyright, market, sell (online and traditional methods), price, print, and distribute a book anywhere in the world, no matter what book format you're working with: ebooks, paperbacks, hardcovers, even audiobooks.

In this book, we're going to focus on *online* advertising, sales, and marketing, alone. And, my introverted friends, I've got some good news and some bad news for you in this regard:

- **Let's start with the bad news**

  If you want your book to sell well, you have to be an active participant in the selling process. There is no way around this, no matter which book publishing business model you've published your book through: the traditional trade publishers, the vanity publishers, or the hybrid publishers. Authors are entrepreneurs. Your book is your business.

- **And now for the good news**

  It is possible to sell your book all around the world using nothing more than a comfortable chair in your quiet writing room, a laptop, an Internet connection, and your own God-given talent for writing.

Need more convincing when I say that *you* have to be an active participant in the selling of your book for it to be truly successful? Okay.

Let's talk about a well-known, bestselling book series you've no doubt heard of: *Chicken Soup for the Soul* by Jack Canfield. In *The Secret* (Byrne, 2006), Jack discussed what it took for him to make his trade-published *Chicken Soup* book a success. Around the time he was first published, he said he was earning only eight thousand dollars per year. Then he went on to share with Byrne,

> . . . so I said, "I want to make a hundred thousand dollars in a year." Now, I had no idea how I could do that. I saw no strategy, no possibility, but I just said, "I'm going to declare that, I'm going to believe it, I'm going to act as if it's true, and release it." So I did that.
>
> About four weeks into it, I had a hundred-thousand-dollar idea. It just came right into my head. I had a book I had written, and I said, "If I can sell four hundred thousand copies of my book at a quarter each, that'd be a hundred thousand dollars." Now, the book was there, but I never had this thought. (One of the secrets is that when you have an inspired thought, you have to trust it and act on it.) I didn't know how I was going to sell four hundred thousand copies.
>
> Then I saw the *National Enquirer* at the supermarket. I had seen that millions of times and it was just background. And all of a sudden it jumped out at me as foreground. I thought, "If readers knew about my book, certainly four hundred thousand people would go out and buy it." About six weeks later I gave a talk at Hunter College in New York to six hundred teachers, and afterward a woman approached me and said, "That was a great talk. I want to interview you. Let me give you my card." As it turns out, she was a freelance writer who sold her stories to the *National Enquirer*. The theme from "The Twilight Zone" went off in my head, like, whoah, this stuff's really working. That article came out and our book sales started to take off. (pp. 96–97)

There are a couple of reasons for sharing this story with you that have nothing to do with spirituality or the lessons taught in *The Secret*. First and foremost, it clearly illustrates the realities of the traditional book publishing industry and just how small a royalty unknown trade-published authors can expect to earn from their books. (Only 25¢ per copy? Ouch! He would have to sell *four hundred thousand copies* of his book in order to earn his goal of $100,000? Yikes!) Second, this story also proves what I've been telling authors all along—that it's up to *you* to sell your own book, no matter which type of publisher you're working with: traditional trade publishers, vanity publishers, or supportive self-publishing houses.

Jack Canfield is the main reason why Jack Canfield became a bestselling author—*not* Jack Canfield's publisher. Repeat that to yourself again. And again. And again. Until it sticks.

Once he got the ball rolling, Jack's book sold millions of copies. And now? Years later, just his name can sell his books without that much effort on his part, no matter whom he publishes through. But he was the one who got that ball rolling in the beginning—much more so than his publisher. His publisher simply produced a professional, saleable version of his book for him and then supplied the distribution networks where Jack could direct people to buy it. Period. The same can be said for *Fifty Shades of Grey*, a vanity-published book by E. L. James that went viral via social media marketing and was later picked up by a subdivision of Random House, a trade publisher that wanted a cut of those sales (Wikipedia, 2015d). And the same can be said for what will need to happen to get the ball rolling for *your* book.

Even if you decide to hire a publicist as yet another vehicle to increase the exposure of your book through the mainstream media (which we will discuss as an option later on), you still have to be able to explain the many virtues of your book's topic matter to the publicist's company so they can explain those virtues to the media on your behalf. You have to first sell it to your publicity firm before it can convince the media to pick up the story.

Once you can reconcile yourself to this fact and commit yourself to actively selling your own book, you've already won half the battle right there. You've put yourself in the driver's seat and are well on your way to success as an author as a direct result. Now let's dig in a little deeper to learn exactly how you're going to do this in an introvert-friendly way.

I CAN SELL AUDIOBOOKS, EBOOKS, PAPERBACKS, AND HARDCOVERS ONLINE?

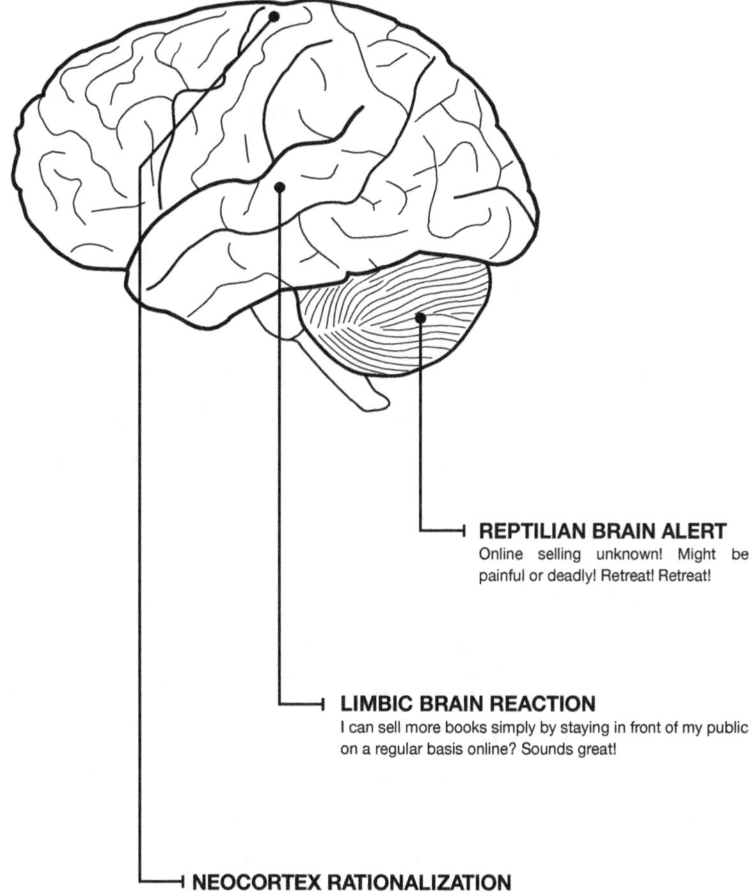

What an amazing world we live in nowadays. You can sell audiobooks, ebooks, paperbacks, and even hardcover books online; this opens you and your book up to a *worldwide* audience, no matter where you're starting from. The Internet is the great equalizer. Webpages are the new storefronts. Money is less necessary to make those storefronts appealing to potential customers than creativity is, but some fundamentals remain. You must drive traffic to your storefront on a consistent basis, and your webpage—whichever one you use, and we'll discuss a few different examples in this book—must catch the attention of your customers in whichever way speaks to them most clearly. Otherwise, they won't bother to browse or make a purchase. They'll pass by your webpage without a second glance, just as they would walk by a dull storefront in a regular shopping mall.

To take the storefront/shopping mall analogy a bit further, there's a very good reason why the top businesses advertise their products and services on a clear and consistent basis. It's because they each know their target market is a fluid and ever-changing stream of old and new customers. There can be hundreds, even thousands, of people flowing through a shopping mall past all the shoe stores, clothing stores, furniture stores, et cetera, on any given day. Everyone has a need to buy shoes, clothing, and furniture at some point in time, but they may not need any of those items *today*. It may be another six months (or more) before they're actually in the market for a particular product or service; and, when that day comes, they will have a variety of options to choose from.

So, how does any author survive—or, preferably, *thrive!*—in such a competitive marketplace filled with so many attractive storefronts offering so many types of books in so many different formats? How can you ensure that both old and new customers will click on *your* book's webpage when they're in the market for your particular type of book? There are three things that will dramatically improve your chances of attracting those sales opportunities as they come:

• Top-of-Mind Awareness (TOMA)

Just as it is for businesses inside a shopping mall, your target market is a fluid and ever-changing stream of old and new customers that you need to stay in front of so that when they're ready to buy whatever type of book it is you're selling, they'll recall *your* book ahead of all the others. In the world of advertising, sales, and marketing, this is known as creating top-of-mind awareness (Wikipedia, 2015h).

Some of the traditional ways that businesses create top-of-mind awareness are to place regular ads on television, radio, and billboards, or in print media outlets such as magazines and newspapers. Repetition is the key to success in any advertising campaign, and this can get pretty expensive in these traditional arenas. We're talking hundreds, maybe even thousands, of dollars per month to run enough ads to achieve top-of-mind awareness with the general public, depending on how large a trading area you're trying to reach. Luckily, authors have a virtually free online alternative known as blogging that utilizes the power of keywords to draw people in from anywhere in the world that has Internet access; they also have the benefit of free social media websites to super-charge those blogging campaigns.

In addition to cost-effectiveness, possibly the greatest benefit to blogging and social media marketing is that they are *unobtrusive* forms of advertising. Whereas traditional advertising methods (e.g., print media, television, radio, and billboards) try their best to "interrupt" customers into noticing them, blogging appeals to the audience that is already in the market for your prardocuts and services. No need to try to interrupt anyone to gain his or her interest; if he or she is typing those keywords into a search engine to try to find you, it's because he or she is already interested in what you have to offer. All you have to do is to be there in the top organic search engine results, and voilà: you've got your prospective customer's attention and hopefully some new business to go with it.

So, the first thing you need to do to give your book the best chance at getting noticed is to create top-of-mind awareness by staying in front of all your prospective customers as much as possible. In this book, we'll discuss many ways you can do this from the comfort of your own home, with little or no financial investment. We'll also discuss some other ways that cost a bit more that you may also consider.

• An Attractive, Accessible Storefront

All your blogging and social media marketing efforts will be profitless unless you're using those vehicles to consistently redirect people to the webpage where they can buy your book. We live in an "instant soup" society filled with customers that want quick and easy solutions to their problems. So, make it quick and easy for them to find the place to buy your book once they've read that compelling blog post or viewed that interesting tweet on Twitter. And make the page so attractive, they will want the book even more.

• Convenient, User-friendly Purchase Options

Some people are more comfortable with online shopping than others are. Where one customer may want to pay for a purchase using PayPal (2015), another will prefer to pay via the credit card of their choice. And there are still those individuals who would really appreciate an old-fashioned "pay by cheque or money order" option. As such, the more purchase options you can provide, the more convenient and user-friendly your online storefront will appear. It's the equivalent of casting a much wider net to catch a greater variety of fish.

Perhaps it's easier to comprehend selling audiobooks and ebooks online because they are digital files (also sometimes referred to as "soft copies") that can be downloaded onto a computer or handheld device for listening and viewing. Most people don't think about paperbacks and hardcovers in the same way. They view these files only as the final printed "hard copy" versions of themselves but the truth is, even paperbacks and hardcovers begin as digital files before they ever reach a print house.

It used to be that whenever a book was published, there was automatically a large run of 1,000 or more copies of it printed and stored away in a large warehouse by the publisher and/or its distributor(s). This large run meant a higher upfront cost for that publisher on all of its books without any guarantee that they would be able to sell them all.

Times have changed. Today's self-publishing authors have many more choices available to them. If they want to print that many books straight away, they still can. Alternatively, they can choose to print fewer numbers of books at a time (i.e., 250 copies) as selling opportunities arise. Yet another alternative is that authors can even choose *not* to print any physical copies of their books at all; instead, they can simply sell copies of them online using an ecommerce website that utilizes Print on Demand (POD) technology. The sky is the limit nowadays, and this is good news for authors everywhere—whether you self-published or produced your book through a traditional trade publisher.

Wikipedia (2015f) provides a great description of what Print on Demand (POD) is and how it works:

Print on demand (POD) is a printing technology and business process in which new copies of a book (or other document) are not printed until an order has been received, which means books can be printed one at a time. While 'build to order' has been an established business model in many other industries, 'print on demand' developed only after digital printing began because it was not economical to print single copies using traditional printing technology such as letterpress and offset printing.

For the authors who don't want to spend extra money on printing and storage but would still like to sell their books in paperback or hardcover formats online, the good news is that it *is* possible. You simply need to create your own webpage (storefront) on an ecommerce website that offers this POD option and then upload your digital files for that book directly to that site using its publishing tools.

There's only one downside to this innovation. As POD technology is still somewhat in its infancy, these specialty presses have only been designed to handle certain printing specifications. Eventually, I'm sure the technology will evolve and be available for all book sizes and types. Until then, authors are somewhat limited to the standard trim sizes—6 x 9 inches, 7 x 10 inches, or 8.5 x 11 inches—and only a few other options.

And what about the authors that have a large run of books already printed and collecting dust in a storage unit? I'm sure you're asking yourselves, "Is it possible for me to sell *these* books online?" The answer is yes, and we'll use this as one of our sample scenarios throughout this book in order to teach you how to do it. Where there's a will, there's a way for every author out there that is determined and willing to take an active role in selling his or her own book.

THE IMPORTANCE OF SETTING GOALS AND STICKING TO THEM

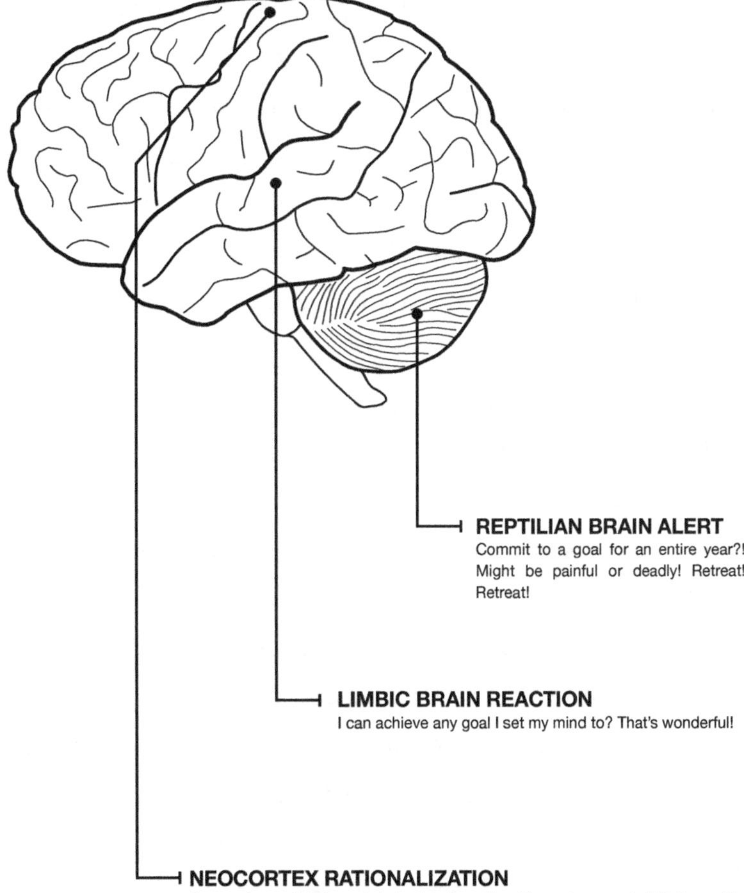

Make this commitment to yourself today: "I'm going to dedicate at least one hour per day, six days per week for the next full year, toward the online advertising, sales, and marketing of my book. No matter what happens, I *will* spend a minimum of six hours per week, every single week for the next full year, toward the online advertising, sales, and marketing of my book. I promise this to myself." This is a small commitment of time that is totally doable. Agreed? (It goes without saying that you can commit to even more time if you wish, but I'll say it anyway.)

I set goals for every single one of my books, and I attach strong emotions to each of those goals. Why do I do this? Because the only way to reach a destination is to first figure out where you're going; and if you give yourself a compelling enough reason to get there that *really* excites your senses, you'll be that much more committed to making it happen. The rest (the hows) always seem to fall into place once you've made that firm decision inside your mind.

It's not for me to advise you what your goal should be nor why you should want to achieve it. That's a very personal thing that is different for every person and every book. It's entirely your choice. My intention is simply to plant some seeds of possibility in your mind, to get you thinking about where and how you might increase the sales of your book online in a way that works well with your introverted personality. Achieve one goal for yourself, and you'll be fearless about setting and achieving more in the future because you'll know you can do it. You'll have proven it to yourself.

On that note, here are four sample books, published in four different formats, for which I've created some example sales and marketing plans that can be used to advertise these books online. I've started by setting a goal for each book, in this chapter, as to what its author may wish to achieve this year, along with his or her compelling "why."

SAMPLE NON-FICTION BOOK GOALS

Self-published ebook cookbook titled *The Cheesecake Doctrine*

This ebook was self-published on KoboBooks.com with worldwide geographic rights (meaning it is available for sale around the world in Kobo's .EPUB format through any of Kobo's various applications and devices such as desktops, ereaders, tablets, IOS, Android, Blackberry, and Windows). The royalty rate the author can expect to earn from KoboBooks (Kobo, 2015) is 70 percent of the listed retail price she has chosen for her book, so she has set it at $34.99 CDN for an expected gross profit of roughly $24.50 CDN per book. (She has converted that price to match the currency in each country where she's selling this book: for example, it sells for $28.99 USD in America, £18.77 GBP in the United Kingdom, and EUR 25.83 in France based on today's market prices.)

As a Canadian girl who sets her goals in Canadian prices, she plans to sell 20 copies of this ebook every month this year so she can earn the equivalent of $490 CDN per month in gross profit (for a total sale of 240 ebooks at $5,880 CDN for the year). She plans to use this extra income to pay for a long-desired tropical vacation in Bora Bora next year. She's wanted to go to Bora Bora since she could remember!

Self-published paperback self-help book titled *Quick and Easy Hairstyling Tips for Teens*

This paperback was self-published on Amazon's CreateSpace.com for distribution on Amazon.com throughout the United States alone. The royalty rate the author can expect to earn when pricing this book at $8.99 USD is $2.34 USD per book after the distributor's cut and other fees such as POD printing costs are first deducted (CreateSpace, 2015).

This author plans to sell 100 copies of this paperback every month this year so she can earn $234 per month in gross profit (for a total sale of 1,200 paperbacks at $2,808 USD for the year). She plans to donate this income to her local youth homeless shelter to help provide the basic necessities of life for its teenage residents as they struggle to complete their educations. She's always been grateful to the family who provided these things to her while she went through hairdressing school, and now she wants to pay it forward.

SAMPLE FICTION BOOK GOALS

Fictional novella audiobook titled *The Path Less Worn*

This fictional novella is based on an inspirational true story about a thirty-year-old man who overcame incredible odds to build a successful health supplement business from humble beginnings as an underprivileged orphan. It was originally produced as a professional quality pocketbook paperback and ebook by a supportive self-publishing house on behalf of its author. The same company has now helped him convert it into audiobook format, complete with a professional voiceover and high definition soundtrack, and has published it nonexclusively to Audible, Amazon, and iTunes via ACX, an Amazon Platform that will pay royalties for any copies sold (ACX, 2015).

The original 4.37 x 7-inch novella was designed to be carried in one's coat pocket for easy accessibility to inspirational reading even when travelling. Due to the pocketbook format, the author set a "pocketsize" retail price to match it: $4.99 USD per copy for both the ebook and the paperback version. For consistency, the audiobook is priced the same. Based on the publishing agreement in place, the gross profit the supportive self-publishing house, Polished Publishing Group (2015b) will earn by distributing this book online on behalf of this author is 25 percent of the list price, for a total of $1.25 per book. The author, in turn, will take home 40 percent of the $1.25 for a total gross profit of 50¢ per book.

Luckily, because this author published through a supportive self-publishing house, he has retained 100 percent copyright ownership of his entire end product (the words *and* the artwork produced for him in all formats of the title) which allows him more control over where he sells his books and what retail price he chooses to sell them at. As such, this author has also decided to produce and sell CD copies of this audiobook direct from his own website, which is why he granted ACX only a *non*-exclusive contract rather than an *exclusive* contract through his publisher. If he had granted them an exclusive contract, then they would be the only ones who could sell his book online. Not even he, himself, could sell them direct elsewhere. By contrast, because he has retained his right to sell his audiobooks direct through his own website's storefront, he will take home 100 percent of the profits from the directly sold copies: $4.99 per book. No middlemen to pay.

What a difference in gross profit on the copies he sells direct! A much better margin, indeed! But it always helps to have extra distributors (particularly distributors with trusted brands) to help sell one's books. Having an audiobook available for sale through Apple iTunes definitely lends even more credibility to the book, and the author recognizes that.

On that note, this author has a goal to sell 1,000 copies of this audiobook every single month: He will sell 50 percent of them through Audible, Amazon, and iTunes at an expected gross profit of 50¢ USD per book, for a total of $250 USD per month; he'll sell the other 50 percent of them direct at $4.99 USD per book, for a total of $2,495 per month. The grand total per month for those 1,000 books is $2,745 USD in gross profit. (The grand total per year for those 12,000 audiobooks is $32,940 in gross profit).

This author's compelling "why" is that he would love to continue working as a travelling health supplement salesman, inspirational speaker, and author, living life on his own terms rather than being chained to a nine-to-five desk job. This book is yet another new revenue stream for a business he loves and feels so passionate about and that allows him to inspire and empower others to achieve their own dreams, just as he and the protagonist in his fictional novella did.

Limited edition hardcover children's book about adoption titled *A Family for Bailey*

This limited edition hardcover book was originally published and printed by a traditional trade publisher 10 years ago. Because it was trade published, the publisher owned the copyright of the book and paid this author only a small 8 percent royalty on the list price of $25 CDN, for a total of $2 CDN in gross profits per book for that author over the past decade. The copyright ownership of this title has now reverted back to the author, as per the original publishing contract. Five hundred unsold copies of the original 1,000-copy print run have been returned to the author from the publisher's warehouse, and he is storing them in his garage. It's now his responsibility to sell them. Luckily, because 100 percent copyright ownership has now returned to him, he will also enjoy 100 percent gross profits on all the copies he sells direct.

These are high-quality, limited edition hardcovers—priceless keepsakes for adopted children and their adoptive families to commemorate their special bonds. This author has decided to sell the remaining books at the original recommended retail price of $25 CDN each (for a total of 500 hardcovers at $12,500 CDN for the year), and he plans to put these profits into savings for his own cherished adopted child to use toward her college education.

Throughout this book, we'll build on these four examples by discussing some of the best online selling options available to these introverted authors to help them achieve their goals. This is not an exhaustive list, but it will give you a really good start toward your own advertising, sales, and marketing plan using some common websites that you may already be familiar with. It will plant those seeds of possibility in your mind.

On that note, here is a space for you to calculate the gross (before taxes) profit of your own book based on where you had it published and in what format it was published. What is the current retail price of your book? What portion of that retail price can you expect to be paid in royalties? Or will it be a direct profit? Get specific here:

____

____

____

____

____

____

____

____

____

And here is another space for you to write your goal for that book as to where you want to go (your destination in terms of number of copies you wish to sell per month and the gross profit that will translate into), along with your own compelling reason why you want to achieve this:

____

____

____

____

____

____

____

____

This chapter began with you making the following commitment to yourself: "I'm going to dedicate at least one hour per day, six days per week for the next full year, toward the online advertising, sales, and marketing of my book. No matter what happens, I *will* spend a minimum of six hours per week, every single week for the next full year, toward the online advertising, sales, and marketing of my book. I promise this to myself." Now let's talk about what you're actually going to do during those six hours every week.

- **Initial week (after you've read this book in full)**

  These first six hours can be spent setting up your storefront, blog site, and other various social media sites (such as PayPal, a blogging site like EzineArticles and/or your own website, Facebook, Twitter, LinkedIn, and YouTube accounts) if you haven't already done so.

- **Every week after that for the next year**

  You will dedicate, on average, four hours toward writing and posting at least two 500-word blog entries per week. You'll spend the other two hours toward effectively sharing these blog entries (and various other posts) online via social media. You can divide up this time however you want to during the week so it fits best with your schedule.

That's it, that's all. Totally doable. Agreed?

I'll share something else with you now: my personal goal for *this* book. As I mentioned earlier in this book, it had been my goal to become a bestselling author since as far back as I could remember. In 2013, I achieved that goal on two different levels: first, by having two of my books publicly listed as bestsellers on Amazon in both Canada and the United States; and second, by having one of those two books also publicly listed as a bestseller in a prominent daily newspaper in Calgary, Alberta, Canada. By 2014, after the publication of my next book, I was soon publicly listed as an Amazon bestseller in the United Kingdom, too.

Now it's time to take it to the next level. I want this book to be publicly listed as a *national* bestseller in a prominent national publication. To become a national bestseller, I will sell 10,000 copies of this book through the booksellers across the country that report their book sales to the country's leading organization for creating official bestseller lists for the major publications. Doing so will produce a gross profit (royalty through PPG) for me of roughly $40,000 CDN.

The number one reason why this goal is so emotional for me is because it is the continuation of a childhood dream realized, which gives me such a strong sense of pride and accomplishment all in itself. But, as the years pass and I grow more as a person, I've learned that it is just as fulfilling—if not *more* fulfilling—to help other authors achieve their goals, too. I can really, truly help other introverted authors through the lessons in this book. And the idea of helping 10,000 of them become more successful by showing them how they can increase their book sales—just as I have—fills my heart with immense joy.

So, that's my goal. There it is. I've put it out there now, so I *must* achieve it. The sense of urgency to prove myself right is a strong one!

PRICE-BASED MARKETING VERSUS VALUE-BASED MARKETING

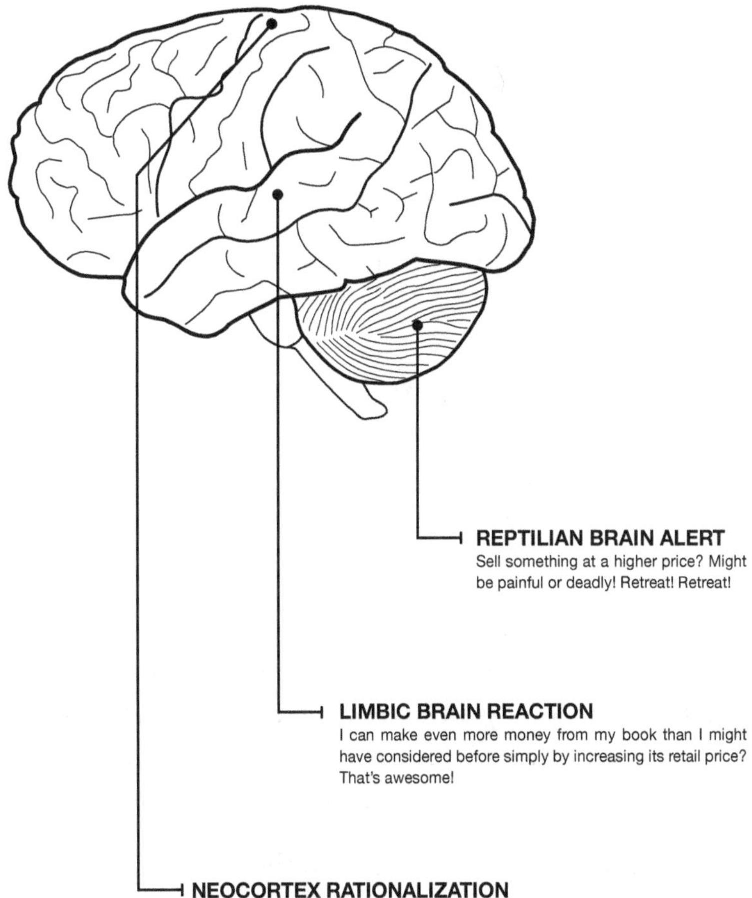

I've received several emails via LinkedIn, over the years, from newly self-published authors who were advertising their books, trying to convince me to buy them. If you're one of these authors, I genuinely applaud you for taking that important step toward self-promotion. Good for you! But now I'm going to tell you why I (and probably most of the other people you sent that email to) never bought your book. It's because your message was flawed in one or, perhaps, all of the following ways. Not to worry, though. I'll teach you a more effective approach to writing (and speaking) your message when we talk about elevator pitches a little later on.

• WIIFM: What's In It for Me?

One of the very first acronyms I learned when I entered the world of sales was WIIFM, which stands for "What's In It for Me?" (UrbanDictionary.com, 2015). My sales coach told me this is what all our customers are asking themselves, whether consciously or unconsciously, whenever they consider making a purchase. As salespeople, we need to be aware of this acronym and be sure we're answering that question for customers, in all our marketing materials, in a clear and concise manner that speaks to them in their language.

When I say "clear" I mean tell them what's in it for them in a manner that addresses their needs directly. Will your book increase their joy? If yes, how? Will your book decrease their pain? If yes, how? (When you clearly address someone's joy and/or pain, you are appealing to their emotional limbic brains more effectively.)

When I say "concise" I mean tell them what's in it for them in as few words as possible. As I stated earlier, we live in an "instant soup" society, filled with customers that want quick and easy solutions to their problems. The *only* instance when anyone will take the time to read through paragraph after detailed paragraph of promotional material will be if they've picked up that material to read it by their own choice—*not* if they've been "interrupted" by it in an unsolicited email message. Fair enough? (When you are concise in your messaging, you are appealing to their logical neocortex more effectively.)

When I say speak to them in their language, I mean tell them what's in it for them in a manner that they will understand and appreciate most, which brings me to the primary focus of this chapter: to discuss two different marketing "languages" you might choose from to communicate with your prospective customers. There is price-based marketing, and there is value-based marketing. Both have their time and their place, no matter what it is that you're selling.

• Price-Based Marketing

Walmart is one of the most common North American examples of a retailer that uses price-based marketing, also sometimes referred to as the Everyday Low Price (Wikipedia, 2015c) pricing strategy, to sell its products. As soon as I use that retail name, most people understand what I mean without much further explanation. Price-based marketing revolves around selling things for the cheapest price. It appeals to the audience that wants "the best deal" at the lowest possible price, regardless of its brand name or quality.

You speak to a price-based audience with phrases such as "Have what you want for less" and "The affordable solution for thrifty consumers."

• Value-Based Marketing

Prada, by contrast, is an example of a worldwide luxury retailer that uses value-based marketing (Wikipedia, 2015i) to sell its products. As soon as I use that brand name, the concept is once again clear to most people. Value-based marketing revolves around selling things at prices commensurate with the highest quality. It appeals to the audience most concerned with workmanship, expertise, long-term durability, and image—and who can, and will, willingly pay more for it.

You speak to a value-based audience with phrases such as "Sophistication and classical style for discerning women" and "Crafted with care for the distinguished gentleman."

These are two extreme examples, taken from one end of the spectrum to the next, to illustrate the differences between these two marketing languages. Not all price-based marketers will price things as low as Walmart does; nor will all value-based marketers price things as high as Prada does. In fact, the same concepts are used to sell many other things all along that spectrum, including coffee (Dunkin' Donuts versus Starbucks), food (McDonalds versus Fatburger), and cars (Honda Civic versus BMW 3 Series Sedan). The main point here is that the wording you use to speak to a price-conscious audience will be very different from the wording you use when you speak to a value-conscious audience. The other point is that you can apply either price-based marketing or value-based marketing to everything and anything you're selling—including all types and formats of books. It all depends on your customers' wants and needs.

Think about your own buying habits for a moment. There are probably some things you purchase based on the lowest price (e.g., maybe the paper towels you use in your kitchen, or the basic office products you use in your home office); and there are probably some other things you will gladly pay extra for (e.g., perhaps that new dining room set you plan to entertain guests with for years to come, or the extracurricular activities your kids are begging you to let them join that could turn into a lucrative career for them down the road).

When you're thinking about which marketing strategy will work best to sell your book, you need to take a couple of key things into account.

The first thing you need to ask yourself is, "What is most important to my readers: The best price or the best value?" The second thing you need to consider is how much profit you want to earn from your book. Obviously, the higher you price it, the better your profit margin will be. But if the higher price doesn't match with your readers' core values, then you won't make the sale. These two things need to be in sync.

Do you offer the best value? Or do you offer the best price? Decide who you are early on—what the core intention of your book truly is—and then be true to that vision through and through. Understand your target market—your customers' preference—*before* you design your advertising, sales, and marketing strategy; and then make sure that that strategy is consistent with their preference in every single way, including the retail price you've set for every format of your book and the messaging you use to sell it. You'll sell far more books over the long run if you do this.

Be clear. Be concise. Be consistent.

SAMPLE NON-FICTION BOOK MARKETING STRATEGIES

Self-published ebook cookbook titled *The Cheesecake Doctrine*

The author of *The Cheesecake Doctrine* has decided to sell her ebook cookbook using value-based marketing.

The audience she has decided to target with this book is primarily adult females, both homemakers and self-employed caterers all over world, between the ages of 25 and 55 with an average, combined annual household income of more than $85,000 CDN (and the equivalent in other countries). Her customers love to entertain guests with delicious, artistic treats and desserts. That said, they are also very busy with children and other work in their day-today lives, so she wants to appeal to how overwhelming that feels at times (pain) and offer them a quick and easy solution (joy) by replacing all their tattered, old, cheesecake recipe books with one sleek, new, searchable ebook.

While many of her competitors are selling ebooks for $9.99 CDN or less, this author will have to be diligent in promoting the true value of her book in order to make any sales at $34.99 per copy: For example, $34.99 CDN for one ebook recipe book that replaces over $250 worth of tattered, old dessert cookbooks? When it's positioned that way, doesn't it sound like a great value? Indeed!

Self-published paperback self-help book titled *Quick and Easy Hairstyling Tips for Teens*

The author of *Quick and Easy Hairstyling Tips* for Teens has decided to sell her paperback using price-based marketing.

The audience she has decided to target is teenage girls and boys between the ages of 13 and 19, along with their parents, throughout the United States. The main emphasis of her book is to save them time and money by showing them some quick and easy do-it-yourself ways to style their own hair for special events such as job interviews, dates, graduation ceremonies, weddings, et cetera. Rather than paying $25+ per each hair style at a professional salon, now they just have to pay $8.99 USD once for the same ongoing results—a tremendous savings over time.

The second underlying theme of her marketing campaign is philanthropy—inviting others to help her support homeless youths all across America through the purchase of her book. This is the primary way she will tug on their heartstrings and appeal to their emotional limbic brains to sell her book.

SAMPLE FICTION BOOK MARKETING STRATEGIES

Fictional novella audiobook titled *The Path Less Worn*

The author of *The Path Less Worn* has decided to sell his fictional audiobook using price-based marketing to keep it consistent with the marketing strategy he used previously when selling the paperback and ebook versions of this title.

The audience he has decided to target is adult males and females aged 20 to 40 located all around North America, who are interested in self-improvement, health supplements, and financial success. These are people much like himself who are tired of "the nine to five grind" of the standard workday (pain), would love to enjoy more success in all areas of their lives (joy), and who also love to read/watch/listen to inspirational stories (joy).

His primary emphasis is to make his encouraging message easily affordable for everyone—even those who are struggling financially, just as he was when he first left the orphanage and started out on his own. He has accomplished this with the $4.99 USD retail price for this book.

Limited edition hardcover children's book about adoption titled *A Family for Bailey*

The author of *A Family for Bailey* has decided to sell his limited edition hardcover book using value-based selling, just as his publisher did for the past ten years. But he will sell his with an added twist—as author-signed copies.

Where most children's books are selling at $12.99 CDN or less, this author will have to effectively explain the true value of this particular children's book in order to sell it at $25 CDN per copy. He does this by targeting all Canadian families with adopted children who are struggling with any possible feelings of rejection or abandonment (pain) and showing them just how real and true their adoptive family's love for them really is (joy).

This is the story of a child who finds a stray dog in his back alley one evening, and who must convince his parents of the value of adopting this animal into their home. Through the child's own love for this dog, it is clear that adoptive love is just as powerful and lasting as biological love is. That's what makes this book so precious and worth every cent of the $25 CDN retail price. It is a keepsake for that child into adulthood—a permanent and tangible reminder of a very special family bond.

Now here is some space for you to write your own marketing strategy for your book. What's in it for your customer? And which language will you use to speak to them: price-based marketing or value-based marketing? Write your answer to these questions here:

____

____

____

____

____

____

____

YOUR CUSTOMERS FIND YOU ONLINE THROUGH KEYWORDS

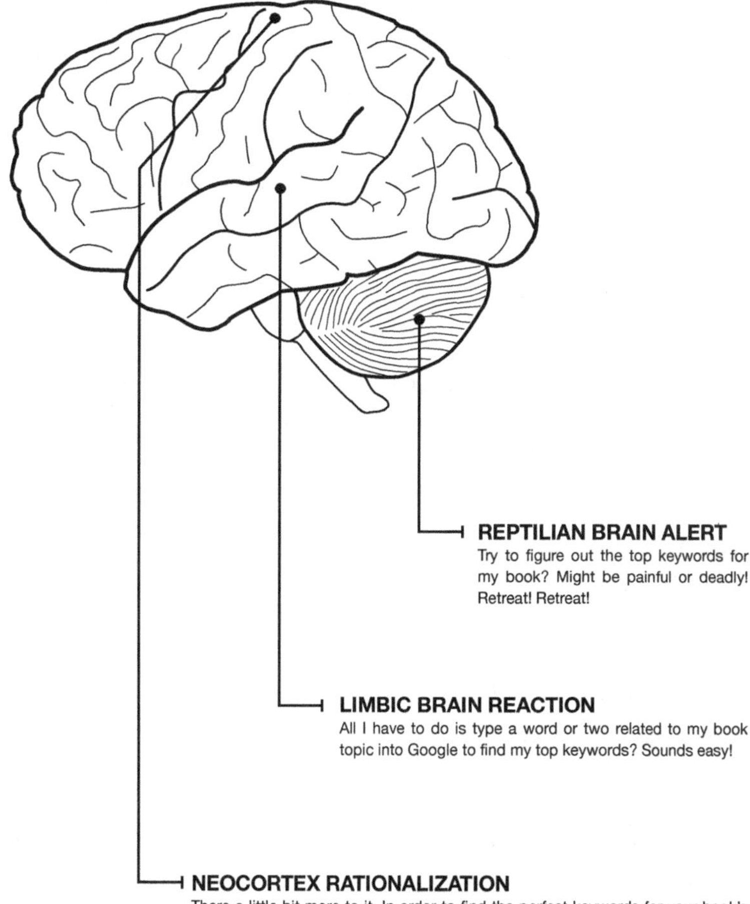

What is a keyword? In short, a keyword is a phrase that someone might type into a search engine such as Google, Bing, or Yahoo to try to find something they're looking for. For example, as the founder and publisher at PPG, I know my company's clientele often "Googles" keywords such as "how to publish a book" and "how to sell a book" to find our types of services; so, I make sure to write blog entries and online articles containing these phrases and then link them to the ecommerce sites where I sell various books on these topics.

Below is a small list of the infinite number of keywords that might be used to sell our sample books. When choosing your own keywords, try to keep in mind the type of book you're selling, the topic(s) of that book, the trading area you want to sell it in (i.e., worldwide, a particular country, a particular state, province, or city), and your chosen marketing language/strategy. This will ensure you reach the right buyers for your book.

SAMPLE NON-FICTION BOOK KEYWORDS

Self-published ebook cookbook titled *The Cheesecake Doctrine*

cheesecake recipe ebook

cheesecake recipes from around the world

best cheesecake recipes in the world

gluten free cheesecake

chocolate cheesecake recipe

unbaked cherry cheesecake

cheesecake lovers

Self-published paperback self-help book titled *Quick and Easy Hairstyling Tips for Teens*

paperback book of hairstyles

youth homelessness in America

hairstyles for teenage guys

hairstyles for teenage girls

quick and easy hairstyles

affordable hairstyles

SAMPLE FICTION BOOK KEYWORDS

Fictional novella audiobook titled *The Path Less Worn*

inspirational audiobooks

orphanages in North America

natural health supplements

orphans in North America

financial success story

self-improvement audiobooks

financial success formula

Limited edition hardcover children's book about adoption titled *A Family for Bailey*

hardcover children's books

Canadian adoption process

Canadian international adoption

emotions during adoption

dogs and children

limited edition collectible books

Now here is some space for you to write out a list of possible keywords for your book:

SELL THE *BENEFITS* OF YOUR BOOK —NOT THE FEATURES

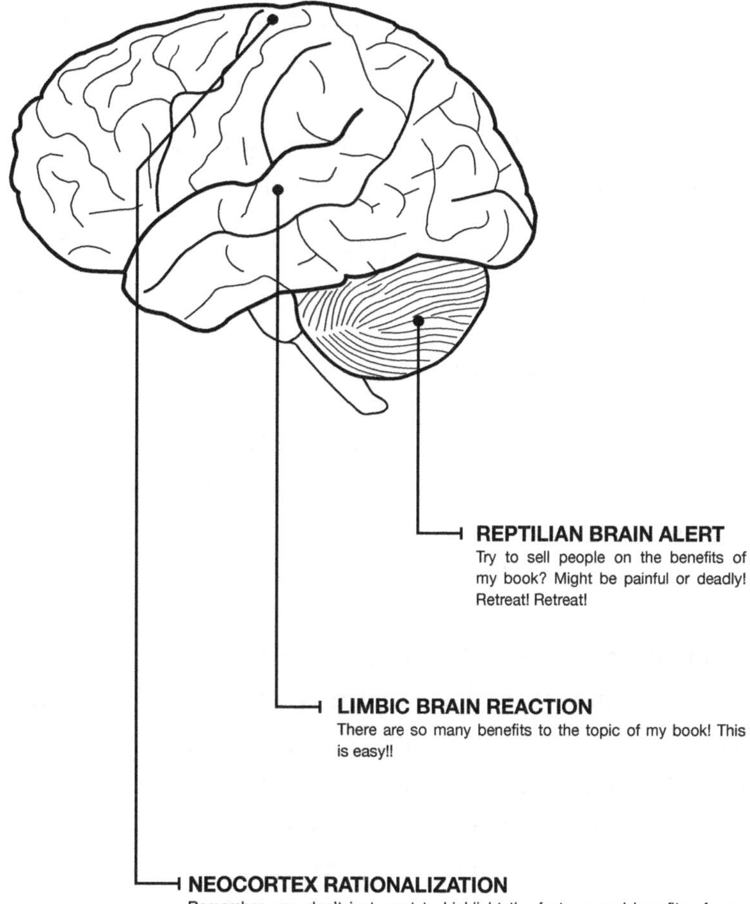

Customers don't buy books so much because they want a book. They buy books because they want a solution of some kind—whether that solution is to entertain themselves, escape from reality for a while, pass the time in an enjoyable way, or learn something new. Marketing campaigns that focus on selling the features of a book ahead of the benefits make the incorrect assumption that their readers will automatically understand why they should buy it. Proper communication of the benefits is crucial to making a sale.

Here's a common example showing the difference between features and benefits:

- **Sells the features of a new pair of gloves**
  Buy our waterproof, breathable, soft-shell work gloves today.

- **Sells the benefits of those features**
  Keep your hands warm and dry while maintaining ease of movement during your entire outdoor work day with these waterproof, breathable, soft-shell gloves.

The first advertisement focuses only on the features of those gloves and assumes that potential customers will understand how a "waterproof, breathable, soft shell" can benefit them. However, what if those customers have just moved to the north from a tropical island, and they have yet to experience a humid, winter climate? What if they haven't worn gloves to do outside handiwork before now? How will they understand the true benefits of these particular features unless you spell them out to them ahead of time? Those customers might not realize it yet, but they aren't merely buying a pair of gloves—what they're buying is the ability to do their job outdoors as comfortably and easily as possible.

Now let's look at the features and benefits of our four sample books. Keep in mind that we're not only looking at the features and benefits of the topic matter of each book, but also the format of the book itself. Each different format has its own unique qualities.

SAMPLE NON-FICTION BOOK BENEFITS

Self-published ebook cookbook titled *The Cheesecake Doctrine*

- **Sells the features of an ebook cookbook**

Buy this digital .EPUB cookbook filled with a wide variety of cheesecake recipes from all around the world.

- **Sells the benefits of those features**

Now a wide variety of cheesecake recipes from all around the world are quickly searchable and at your fingertips, on every digital device from your smartphone to your tablet or computer desktop, in this easy-to-use .EPUB cookbook.

Self-published paperback self-help book titled *Quick and Easy Hairstyling Tips for Teens*

- **Sells the features of a paperback self-help book for teens**

Buy this quick and easy hairstyling guide for teens in an affordable paperback format.

- **Sells the benefits of those features**

Now you can have access to dozens of affordable, quick, and easy hairstyles for teens, with clear step-by-step instructions on the left and matching how-to diagrams on the right, when you prop this paperback up in front of your mirror.

SAMPLE FICTION BOOK BENEFITS

Fictional novella audiobook titled *The Path Less Worn*

- **Sells the features of an audiobook novella**

Buy this inspirational novella, *The Path Less Worn*, in audiobook format today.

- ## Sells the benefits of those features

  Whether you're listening at work, during a jog, on a plane, or in the car, you'll enjoy this inspirational novella so much more with its studio narrated voice-overs and professional music scoring that allows you to truly feel the experience and emotion of the story *The Path Less Worn.*

Limited edition hardcover children's book about adoption titled *A Family for Bailey*

- ## Sells the features of a hardcover children's book about adoption

  Buy this limited edition hardcover children's book about the joys of adoption for your adopted child today.

- ## Sells the benefits of those features

  Gift your adopted child with a meaningful and tangible reminder of your lifelong bond in this author-signed, limited edition, collectable children's book about adoption, *A Family for Bailey.*

When you sit down to design a marketing strategy around who your customers are, what they value most, and how your book best meets their needs (both in topic matter and in format), begin by writing down a list of your book's features, but don't stop there! Dig a little deeper to determine the benefits of those features to consumers. The extra time and effort will make a world of difference to your sales.

Now here is some space for you to write the features and benefits of your book, based on whatever format you have published it in:

____

____

____

____

INCLUDE A CALL TO ACTION IN ALL YOUR MARKETING MATERIALS

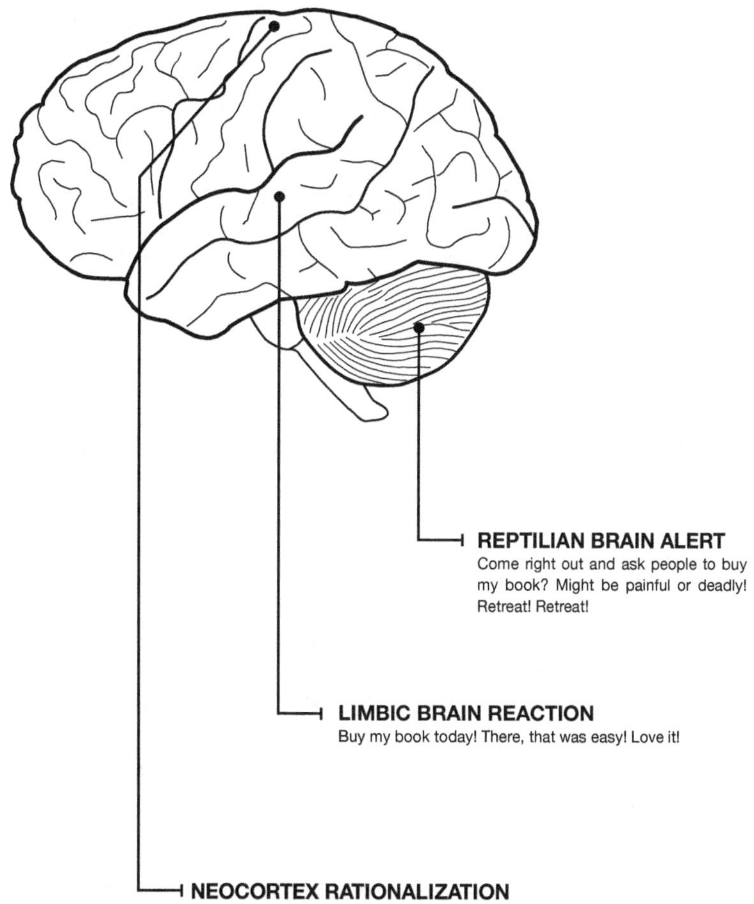

Now let's discuss one of the most obvious, yet least utilized, components of every successful sales campaign: the call to action. Simply stated, a call to action is your very clear request to consumers to buy your book TODAY! Right now!

Sometimes, salespeople do an amazing job of convincing buyers that whatever they're selling is a wonderful thing, but then they let those buyers walk away without actually asking for the sale while the opportunity is still hot. Don't let that opportunity get cold! Come right out and ask for the sale right in the moment. It doesn't work all the time, but it works a lot better than not asking at all—that much I can promise. If you get used to doing this, you'll sell way more books over time.

SAMPLE NON-FICTION BOOK CALLS TO ACTION

Self-published ebook cookbook titled *The Cheesecake Doctrine*

Why wait? Download your copy right now and impress your guests tonight!

Self-published paperback self-help book titled *Quick and Easy Hairstyling Tips for Teens*

Click here to buy a copy, and donate to homeless youths today!

SAMPLE FICTION BOOK CALLS TO ACTION

Fictional novella audiobook titled *The Path Less Worn*

Download this audiobook now so you have it ready when the inspiration hits!

Limited edition hardcover children's book about adoption titled *A Family for Bailey*

Order one while supplies last!

Now here is some space for you to write an effective call to action for your book:

BRING IT ALL TOGETHER IN AN EFFECTIVE ELEVATOR PITCH

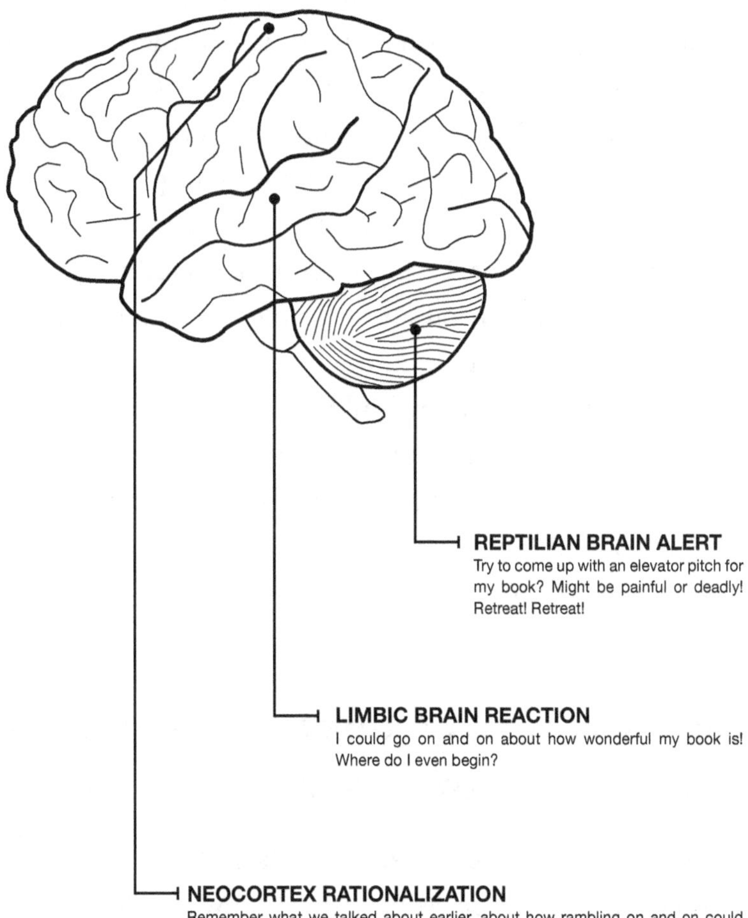

What is an elevator pitch, and why should every author have one memorized and ready to recite at a moment's notice? In short, it is a brief sales pitch that will help you to sell more books both in person and online: According to the Free Dictionary (2015b), "the name 'elevator pitch' reflects the idea that it should be possible to deliver the summary in the time span of an elevator ride, or approximately thirty seconds to two minutes."

When delivered correctly and confidently, it often results in a sale right on the spot. At the very least, it will pique the interest of your audience for future reference so they will think of your book first when they are in the market to buy one on your topic.

An effective elevator pitch should encapsulate everything we've discussed up to this point: it needs to be clear, concise, and consistent with all your other marketing materials, including pricing; it needs to answer the question "what's in it for me?" in a marketing language your customers will understand and appreciate most, and that will elicit an emotional response in their limbic brains; it should include one or two of your top keywords; it should clearly outline the features and benefits of your book; and it should confidently call your customers to action to buy your book immediately.

Now here are some example elevator pitches for our four sample books.

SAMPLE NON-FICTION BOOK ELEVATOR PITCHES

Self-published ebook cookbook titled *The Cheesecake Doctrine*

When only a choice dessert made from the finest ingredients will do, you need *The Cheesecake Doctrine*. Now a wide variety of cheesecake recipes from all around the world are quickly searchable and at your fingertips, on every digital device from your smartphone to your tablet or computer desktop, in this easy-to-use .EPUB cookbook. Extraordinary delights await you from chocolate cheesecake and unbaked cherry cheesecake to an appealing variety of gluten-free treats. Why wait? Download your copy right now and impress your guests tonight!

Self-published paperback self-help book titled *Quick and Easy Hairstyling Tips for Teens*

Why spend $25+ per hair style at a salon when *Quick and Easy Hairstyling Tips for Teens* offers several convenient do-it-yourself hairstyles at home for only $8.99 altogether? Patchy Internet service? No worries! Now you can have access to dozens of affordable, quick, and easy hairstyles for teens, with clear step-by-step instructions on the left and matching how-to diagrams on the right, when you prop this paperback up in front of your mirror.

And that's not all. For every copy of this book that is sold to help teenagers style their own hair for special events such as job interviews, dates, graduation ceremonies, weddings, et cetera, a portion of the proceeds will be given to support youth homelessness in America. Let's help *all* teenagers take a step up in life. Click here to buy a copy, and donate to homeless youths today!

SAMPLE FICTION BOOK ELEVATOR PITCHES

Fictional novella audiobook titled *The Path Less Worn*

Based on a true story about the author's own battles to overcome incredible odds and build a successful health supplement business from humble beginnings as an underprivileged orphan, this is the ultimate in inspirational audiobooks. Are you tired of "the nine to five grind" of the standard workday? Would you love to enjoy more success in all areas of your life, particularly with money? Now you can learn the financial success formula described in this book for only $4.99 USD from someone who understands, firsthand, what it is to struggle and succeed.

Whether you're listening at work, during a jog, on a plane, or in the car, you'll enjoy this inspirational novella so much more with its studio narrated voice-overs and professional music scoring that allows you to truly *feel* the experience and emotion of the story *The Path Less Worn*. Download this audiobook now so you have it ready when the inspiration hits. You'll be so glad you did.

Limited edition hardcover children's book about adoption titled *A Family for Bailey*

A Family for Bailey is the touching tale of a child who finds a stray dog in his back alley, one evening, and who must convince his parents of the value of adopting this animal into their home. Through the child's own love for this dog, it is clear that adoptive love is just as powerful and lasting as biological love is. Through this story, your child will gain insight into your emotions during adoption, along with his or her own, to help further develop your emotional attachment to each other.

Your family is priceless to you. All your children are your greatest treasures. Gift your adopted child with a meaningful and tangible reminder of your lifelong bond in this author-signed, limited edition, collectable children's book about adoption, *A Family for Bailey*. Order one while supplies last. It is a keepsake you and your child will cherish forever.

Notice the differences in the value-based elevator pitches versus the price-based elevator pitches. Notice how these authors don't mention price, whatsoever, in a value sell. They focus on the high quality of the book's content and format—of the value it can bring to the buyer's life. If you want your customers to notice the price, go ahead and mention the price. When you want them to focus on the value, you must sell based on the value alone.

Now here is some space for you to write the elevator pitch for your book:

____

____

____

____

____

____

____

____

____

____

____

YOUR BOOK'S WEBPAGE (STOREFRONT) IS CRITICAL TO YOUR SUCCESS!

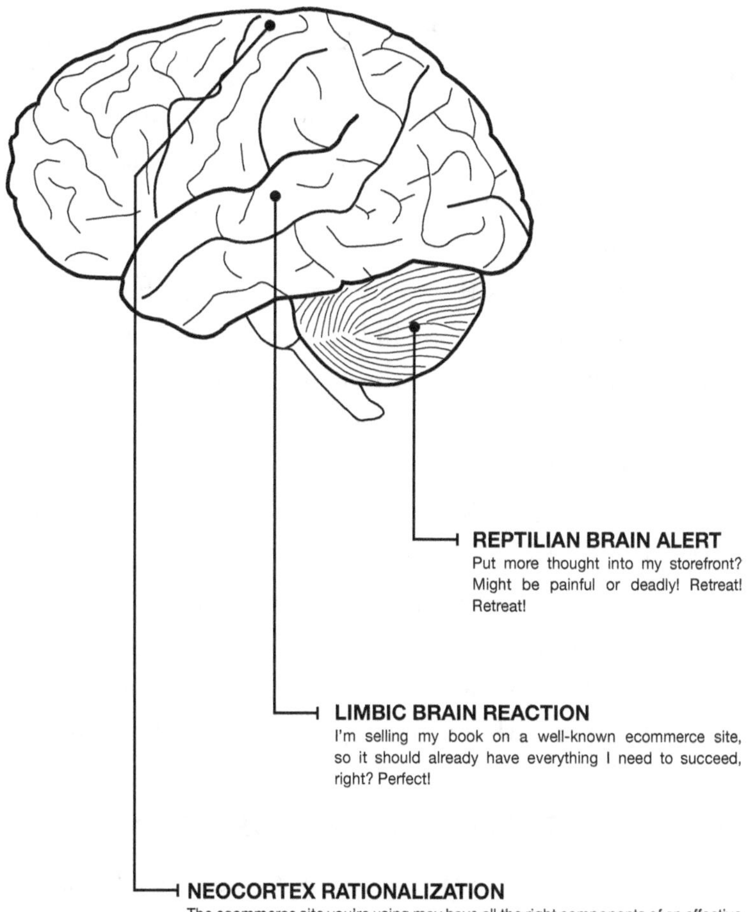

Your online storefront is the webpage people will visit to purchase your book; and, like any other storefront, it must be easily accessible and attractive enough to catch the attention of your customers in a way that speaks to them most clearly. Otherwise, they won't bother to browse or make a purchase. They'll pass by your book without a second glance.

Depending on the publisher you used to produce your book, it may be available for sale on more than one website such as Kobo, Barnes & Noble, Bertram, Gardners, or Amazon to name just a few. For the purpose of this exercise—which is to really focus in on one sales goal for your book—I recommend targeting your efforts on only one storefront, maybe two, at this time. Which one or two should you choose? Well, it depends on what your goal is. For example, in order to become an Amazon bestseller, I had to focus on driving traffic to my various Amazon webpages; and to become a Calgary Herald Bestseller, I had to focus those sales on the local traditional bookstores that feed that particular bestseller list. So, choose one or two storefronts that will help you reach your goal.

What makes an online storefront easily accessible and attractive? It *must* contain all of the following elements: a front cover image of your book; an effective elevator pitch; convenient, user-friendly payment options; and prompt downloading/shipping features that will get your book to your customers quickly. If possible, it's also a great idea to offer a "Look Inside" or "Sneak a Peak" option that allows readers to preview a few pages within the book—a further enticement into buying it.

Now let's look at our four sample books and the different types of storefronts these authors are using to achieve their respective goals.

SAMPLE NON-FICTION BOOK STOREFRONTS

Self-published ebook cookbook titled *The Cheesecake Doctrine*

The beauty of Kobo is that you can publish an ebook on their platform, via their website, in both Adobe .PDF DRM—a type of protection for digital files (Wikipedia, 2015a)—and .EPUB—a type of ebook digital file (Wikipedia, 2015b)— formats. Because the latter is compatible not only with Windows and other computer desktops but also with ereaders, tablets, IOS, Android, and Blackberry, this author has produced her ebook as an .EPUB. She definitely wants her book to be accessible on all these devices in order to reach the largest audience of customers possible.

Another advantage to Kobo is that authors can choose which regions they want to make their books available in all around the world, and they can also choose their own prices for each region in that region's currency. This allows the author of *The Cheesecake Doctrine* to reach her chosen demographic: adult females, both homemakers and self-employed caterers all over world, between the ages of 25 and 55, with an annual household income of more than $85,000 CDN (and the equivalent in other regions' currencies).

Kobo not only allows authors to choose three categories to promote their books in (i.e., Nonfiction, Food & Drink, Baking & Desserts, Cakes/Desserts/Pastry), but it also shows your book's ranking in those three categories at the top of your personal storefront, right beside the picture of your front cover. This helps you to track your sales goal along the way.

Kobo has a "Synopsis" section where you can insert your elevator pitch, an easy-to-locate "Buy" button for making quick purchases, and several payment options such as gift card, credit card, and PayPal. The gift card option is perfect for those who are uncomfortable with putting their banking information online because it allows them to buy a gift card in person, at any of the bookstores affiliated with Kobo, and then make their online purchase with the gift card instead. Kobo's online store also has a "Preview" button customers can click on for a quick look inside the book to see whether they want to buy it;

it also has a section at the bottom where your customers can publish their favourable reviews of your book.

All in all, Kobo's online platform contains all the recommended components of an easily accessible and attractive storefront. It offers an excellent platform for selling ebooks around the world which will help this author to reach her goal.

Self-published paperback self-help book titled *Quick and Easy Hairstyling Tips for Teens*

Amazon's group of sites is one of the most recognized ecommerce websites in the world, and that's a powerful selling tool all in itself. Through its CreateSpace platform, the author of *Quick and Easy Hairstyling Tips for Teens* can upload the digital files for her paperback book's cover and interior directly to Amazon so the book can be printed, bound, and shipped on demand as it sells.

In terms of its storefront, Amazon offers all the same benefits to this author for her paperback book as the Kobo platform offers to the first author for her ebook: a choice of three categories to sell her book in, the ability to target teenagers and their parents throughout the United States, a marketing section where the elevator pitch can be inserted right beside the front cover image of the book, a "Look Inside" feature for a quick glimpse of the content of the book, an easy-to-locate "Add to Cart" button for making purchases, a section where people can write favourable reviews of the book, and all the same payment options that Kobo offers. In addition to that, Amazon has various shipping options available to customers who may want to receive the book a little sooner than others. It has all the recommended components of an easily accessible and attractive storefront for POD paperback books.

SAMPLE FICTION BOOK STOREFRONTS

Fictional novella audiobook titled *The Path Less Worn*

iTunes is one of the most popular audiobook ecommerce websites right now, so this author has decided to focus the majority of his energy on promoting his storefront here, ahead of the two other ACX storefronts: Audible and Amazon. He has also chosen to sell CD copies of this audiobook directly from his own website as he'll not only earn a better profit margin there, but he can also offer more flexible payment options than iTunes offers.

iTunes works the same as Kobo in the sense that buyers can browse the selection of audiobooks right on the itunes.apple.com website (which acts as the primary online storefront); but, rather than there being a "Buy" button displayed, there is a "View in iTunes" button, instead, which redirects buyers to download the iTunes software to whichever device they plan to download the book to. It is from the iTunes platform itself that they can purchase the audiobook.

Each storefront—whether it's the one on the iTunes website or the one on the downloaded iTunes platform where you actually buy/listen to the book—contains the same information. There is room to display the book cover, there is a description field for placing the elevator pitch for the audiobook, there is room for book reviews to be displayed, and books can be quickly and easily downloaded for listening. The only downside is the lack of payment options. Basically, the only way to download anything from iTunes (whether it's through an app on your smartphone, a Netflix show on your Apple TV, or an audiobook for your computer or iPad) is to use whichever payment option you chose when you set up your original Apple iTunes account, way back when. They're all linked together, which some people may find very convenient and others may not.

On the plus side, though, audiobooks are downloadable for buyers to listen to on any number of devices—basically any of the devices they've downloaded iTunes to. It's a very popular platform all over North America: the target market the author *of The Path Less Worn* is trying to reach. So, this is a great place to sell downloadable digital copies of his audiobook.

To sell the CD copies of his audiobook, he has an online store connected to his GoDaddy website (GoDaddy, 2015). GoDaddy online stores are pretty user-friendly to set up, although there is a monthly service cost to keep them up and running. There is room to display the front cover (or, in this case, the CD cover for the audiobook) along with the elevator pitch for that book. Several different types of payment options, from PayPal to credit cards to cheques or money orders, can also be set up along with customized shipping fees, taxation, and special discount offers. It takes some time and effort to get everything set up initially, but GoDaddy has a toll-free support line to help people through the process, if necessary.

Once customers place an order for the CD version of this author's audiobook on his website, an email is immediately sent to him, prompting him to mail out the CD to them right away. The website even helps him track his sales and build a customer contact list. At the end of the day, GoDaddy has a really well-thought-out ecommerce platform that meets all the criteria of an accessible and attractive online storefront for authors. I highly recommend it.

Limited edition hardcover children's book about adoption titled *A Family for Bailey*

For all the same reasons that the author of the CD audiobook chose GoDaddy, the author of this children's book is choosing the same ecommerce storefront to sell *A Family for Bailey* throughout Canada.

Not only can he set up his own customized taxation and shipping options, but he can also choose to sell everything in Canadian currency to his customers. Everything is customizable and can be accessed and controlled from his desktop computer, his laptop, and even his smartphone, using the GoDaddy app—which means he can run his bookselling business from anywhere, at any time, as long as he has Internet access. Luckily, he already had his own PayPal account set up beforehand, so all he had to do was link his online store to that account, and voilà! He's in business!

Now here is some space for you to write about the online storefront(s) you will use to sell your book and what else you may need (i.e., a PayPal account) in order to get started:

____

____

____

____

____

____

____

____

____

REDIRECT TRAFFIC TO YOUR STOREFRONT USING BLOGGING

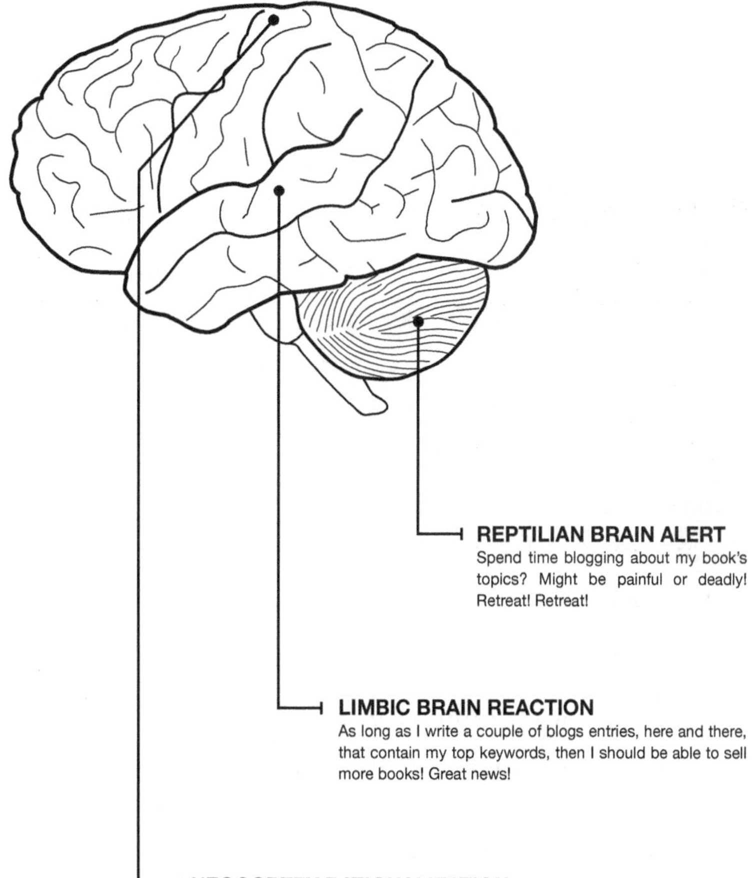

You can use two forms of blogging, also known as online writing for search engine optimization, or SEO (Wikipedia, 2015g), to achieve top-of-mind awareness on the worldwide web and optimize your standing in the search results on search engines such as Google, Yahoo, and Bing: online articles that are written for and posted on high-ranking online publications, and blog entries that are posted to your own website or blog site. Each has its own unique advantage.

- ## Online Articles (Online "Advertorials")

  Some of your keywords (i.e., your business name, your book's title) might have a fairly high search engine ranking. Blogging can help to improve your ranking for *all* of them. The idea is to write several keyword-rich articles—500-word essays that contain the phrases that your customers type into a search engine when they are looking for your particular book topic—and then share those articles with others via email and social media websites. The ultimate goal is for your articles to show up in the top five search results on page one of a search engine because this will dramatically improve the chances of people clicking on them to read them. Obviously, the more articles that are posted online on a regular basis, the better it will work because people will be able to find you via more and more keyword variations.

  Online articles should have an editorial appeal to them that matches the criteria set up by the online publication to which they are being posted. Their primary purpose is to educate people about a certain industry or topic. That said, if you want to increase the sale of your books, then you must also redirect traffic from the advertorial to the online store where people can buy your book. You want them to make that buying decision on the spot while their interest is still hot.

To view samples of these types of articles, visit http://ezinearticles.com/?expert=Kim_Staflund (EzineArticles, 2015). Here, you will see examples specific to the book publishing industry. You'll also see direct links, at the bottom of my author bio page on the site, to the storefronts where two of my related books can be purchased.

- **Blog Entries**

Blog entries are a wee bit different from online articles in that you can say pretty much whatever you want, however you want to say it, because you are posting it to your own page instead of someone else's. Blog entries can be an obvious advertisement for your products, services, events, et cetera, if you choose. You aren't limited by anyone else's content criteria.

A blog site can be a website in its own right, or for businesses, in particular, it can be an extension of one's primary website. For example, PPG's primary website is www.polishedpublishinggroup.com. This is where our customers go to buy book publishing packages from us. The PPG Publisher's Blog is an extension of our primary website: blog.polishedpublishinggroup.com. This is where PPG's founder and publisher blogs and answers industry FAQs (frequently asked questions) about the book publishing industry. Upcoming PPG webinars and workshops are also promoted here.

You can place hyperlinks to your book's storefront throughout each blog entry so readers don't have to go looking for those links on your bio page. This option of blogging is probably the better one for our sample fictional audiobook, *The Path Less Worn*, because its author intends to redirect traffic to more than one storefront: both Amazon's ACX platform and his own website.

- ## Blogging is Word-of-Mouth Advertising on Steroids!

Blogging is a fantastic way to reach more potential buyers more quickly than ever before. Many people, particularly small business owners with fixed budgets, find that word-of-mouth advertising is the best form of advertising for them. This might well be true. When people hear good things about a company from someone they know and trust, they are more apt to trust that company upfront and check it out for themselves.

The only issue with verbal word-of-mouth advertising is that sometimes things get "lost in translation" along the way. Many of us can relate to this by remembering a game we played as children. A dozen or more people sit in a circle together, and a phrase is whispered into the ear of the first person who then whispers it to the next, who then whispers it to the next, and so and on, and so forth. By the time the last person hears the phrase and repeats it aloud for all to hear, it has a completely different context than it did when the first person heard it. With verbal word-of-mouth, word can spread like wildfire, yes—but sometimes the message is distorted along the way.

Blogging, on the other hand, is a written form of word-of-mouth advertising, which means the original message remains intact. Rather than simply speaking about your message, it's the "Share" button at the bottom of an online article or blog entry that enables readers to share your message with others via email and social media websites such as Facebook, Twitter, and LinkedIn to name a few. Imagine that! Imagine how many people are currently using Facebook, Twitter, and LinkedIn, alone; never mind all the other social media sites that are out there today. Imagine how quickly a message can be spread to so many others with the simple click of a "Share" button!

Now, let's look at some sample blogging topics for each of our four example books. You can build your top keywords right into the titles of the advertorial or blog entry for maximum impact. Also, notice how you can piggyback on some really prominent, instantly recognizable keywords anywhere in the world, such as "Marilyn Monroe," to make your story intriguing to an even larger audience.

SAMPLE NON-FICTION BOOK BLOG TOPICS

Self-published ebook cookbook titled *The Cheesecake Doctrine*

How to Download a Cheesecake Recipe Ebook

The History of Cheesecake Recipes from Around the World

Tricks of the Trade: The Best Cheesecake Recipes in the World

How to Make Gluten Free Cheesecake for Celiac Sufferers

How Chocolate Cheesecake Recipes Can Make Halloween More Fun

Deliciously Cool Summer Treats: Five Unbaked Cherry Cheesecake Ideas

240 Chances to Win $240,000! A Mouthwatering Contest for Cheesecake Lovers!

Self-published paperback self-help book titled *Quick and Easy Hairstyling Tips for Teens*

10 Great Reasons to Buy a Paperback Book of Hairstyles for Teens

Five Sobering Facts about Youth Homelessness in America

This Season's Trends: The Most Popular Hairstyles for Teenage Guys

How to Look Your Best for Grad: Fashionable Hairstyles for Teenage Girls

How These Quick and Easy Hairstyles Can Save a Life

Why a Book of Affordable Hairstyles Makes the Best Christmas Gift for Teens

Help Me Support 1,200 Homeless Youths in America This Year: Buy My Book and Enter a Draw to Win Free Haircuts for a Year!

SAMPLE FICTION BOOK BLOG TOPICS

Fictional novella audiobook titled *The Path Less Worn*

How Inspirational Audiobooks Can Complement Your Meditation Sessions

Seven Truths about Orphanages in North America

How Natural Health Supplements Can Improve Your Energy Levels

Why Marilyn Monroe Became One of the Most Successful Orphans in North America

How One Orphan Became an Inspirational Financial Success Story

Five Ways Self-improvement Audiobooks Can Improve Your Life

How One Man's Financial Success Formula Will Change 12,000 People's Lives This Year: Enter this Contest For a Chance to WIN BIG!

Limited edition hardcover children's book about adoption titled *A Family for Bailey*

Three Reasons Why Hardcover Children's Books are Still the Best Gifts for Toddlers

Five Compelling Truths about the Canadian Adoption Process

How to Prepare for the Canadian International Adoption Process

What to Expect: Your Emotions During Adoption

How the Special Bond Between Dogs and Children Can Ease Adoption Anxiety

Only One of These Limited Edition Collectible Books Can Make You a Winner! (Subheading or sidebar: Choose the Right Number and Find a Prepaid Coupon for a Family Weekend at the Banff Springs Hotel inside Your Book!)

Not only are the major keywords for these topics built right into the titles of these blog entries for better searchability on all the search engines, but authors can also use blogging as an opportunity to promote contests, specific to their respective goals, that encourage the sale of the exact number of books they want to sell within a specified time period. Contests can add that extra little incentive to buyers who may be on the fence about choosing this book over another one on the same topic.

If you have a limited budget, you can offer free services like the hairdresser is offering, or you can take out a speciality insurance policy (which usually only costs a couple hundred dollars) to offer a chance at a grand prize of X number of dollars like the author of the ebook cookbook has done here. For those with a little more disposable income, maybe you can prepay a weekend at a luxury hotel and offer that as the grand prize for your contest, like the author of the adoption book has done here. The sky is the limit when you get a little bit creative and think like an entrepreneur.

Now here is some space for you to write the titles of the blogs you're going to write to promote your book along with one specific to a contest you will run to sell your book:

REDIRECT TRAFFIC TO YOUR STOREFRONT USING BOOK REVIEWS

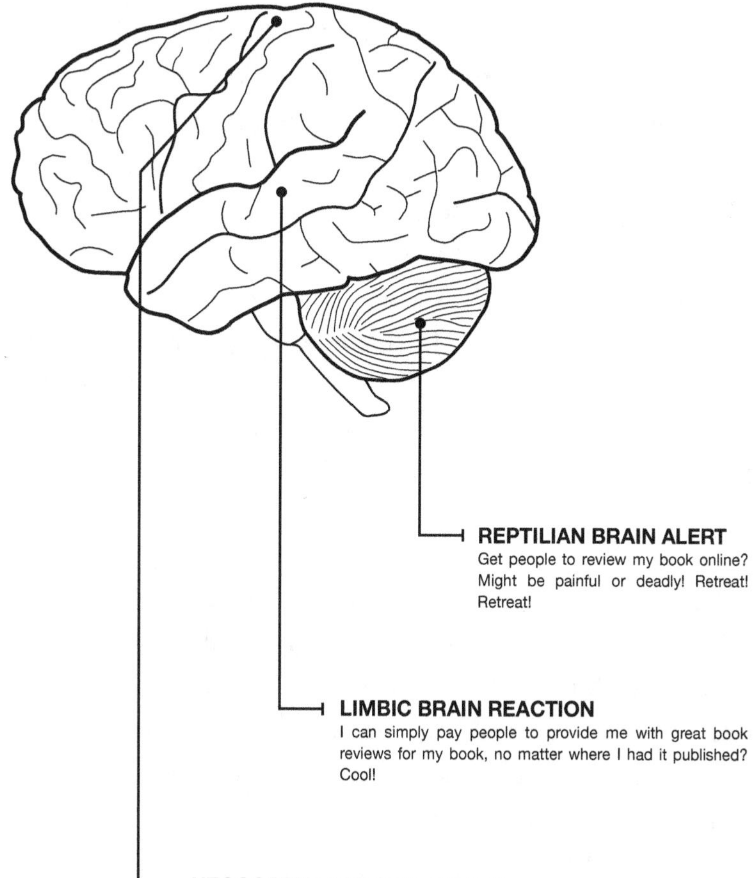

Different types of book reviews are available to help authors sell more books: unpaid traditional book reviews, and paid online book reviews. Each has its own unique pros and cons. Both are effective tools that can be used by authors to sell more of their books.

UNPAID TRADITIONAL BOOK REVIEWS

A common custom among trade publishers that really should be adopted by self-publishing authors is making sure to send out a few complimentary copies of your book to various traditional book reviewers in your area. This is a great way to generate some extra publicity for your book. (We'll discuss publicity and the role of publicists in more detail a bit later on.) The upside is that these reviews are free of charge in the sense that your only cost is the copy of your book and the postage to send it; however, the downside is that you're not guaranteed a review after sending it. It's at the discretion of the reviewer.

Two types of unpaid traditional book reviews are available: one is the review that you send out ahead of time, known as an advance reader copy (ARC), to stir up interest in the book before publication; the other is a published review copy of the actual, final edited version of your book.

- **Advance Reader Copies (ARCs)**

   These unfinished review copies can be printed and mailed out as hard copy galleys or emailed as .PDF files. It is important to ensure they are stamped with the words "Advance Reader Copy (ARC)" on the front cover, and possibly also on every few pages of the interior, to ensure that the reviewer understands the copy is unedited so he or she takes that into account.

- **Published Review Copies**

   When sending a final published review copy to an editor, whether mailed as a hard copy or emailed as a .PDF, make sure to stamp

"Review Copy" on the front cover of the book so it cannot be resold for profit. This also ensures that it will get to the right person at the newspaper or magazine to which you're sending it for review.

A great book review written by a highly respected reviewer within the literary community can do wonders to help boost your book sales in much the same way as other forms of publicity can. When shared via social media, a prize endorsement such as this can catch on as quickly as wildfire. It's definitely worth the cost of a complimentary book or two.

PAID ONLINE BOOK REVIEWS

Paid online book reviews are a fantastic advertising tool for authors. They can aid you in your efforts to direct traffic to the storefront where your book is currently for sale, thereby increasing the chance of a sale. They can also provide you with relevant content that you can share via social media to further promote your book to your followers.

The upside to these types of reviews is that whereas you're not guaranteed a review when you send a book to a traditional book reviewer, you *are* guaranteed a review when you pay for one from a non-traditional book reviewer. The downside is that you must pay for it.

When completed by a reputable organization, these paid reviews are still unbiased reviews—which may be good or bad. Once the review is complete, you are given an opportunity to decline or approve it to be published online for all to see. If you decline it, you won't get your money back; it simply won't be shared publicly at your request. But if you approve it, it might be posted to that reviewer's high-traffic website, posted to your book online, and/or shared with various wholesalers and retailers all around your country (and possibly other parts of world, depending on where you have the book reviewed).

A complimentary paid book review can boost your sales in much the same way a traditional review can. It is definitely worth the investment, in my opinion.

REDIRECT TRAFFIC TO YOUR STOREFRONT USING FACEBOOK

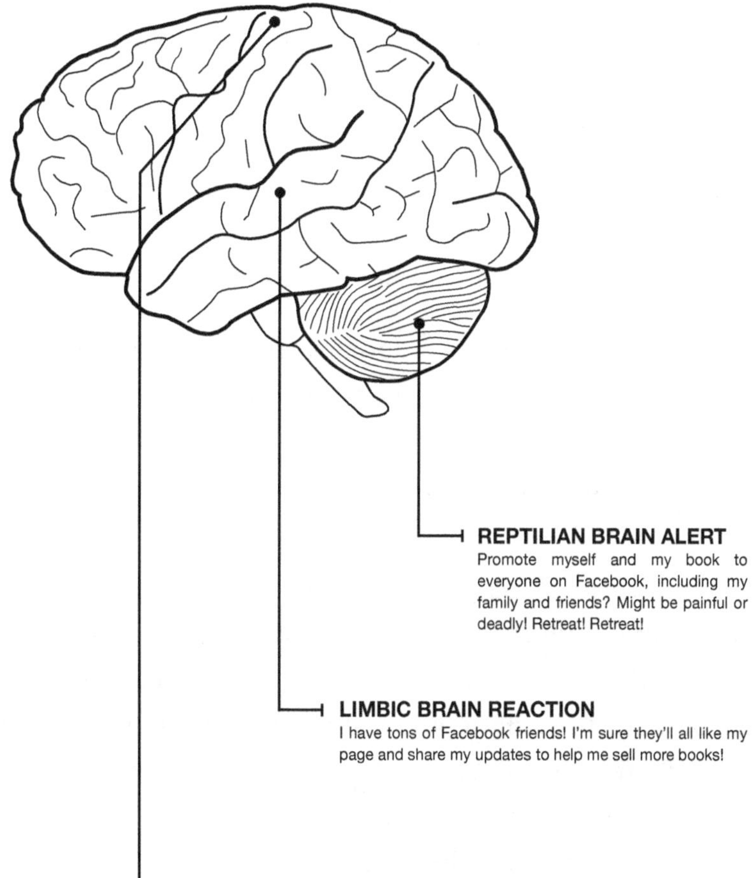

It's probably unnecessary to go too deeply into an explanation about what Facebook is and how to use it, because almost everyone in your country (in this world!) now has a Facebook account if he or she has a Smartphone or personal computer of some kind along with Internet access. The fact that it gives people the potential to reach an audience all around the world makes it a powerful advertising vehicle. The fact that it is free of charge makes it easy for anyone and everyone to use.

There are two ways you can gain interested followers on Facebook (Facebook Help Centre, 2015b): one, you can share updates about yourself with the public via your personal profile; and two, you can promote yourself, your events, and your books via your company page.

If your goal is to represent your business, brand or product on Facebook, create a Page. A Page lets you engage with people on Facebook and offers tools to help you manage and track engagement.

If your goal is to share updates from your personal Timeline with a broader audience, you can allow people to follow you. When you allow people to follow you, anyone on Facebook can follow you to get your public updates in their News Feed, even if you're not friends on Facebook.

Whether it's a page or a personal profile, be sure to fill in the "About" and other sections with information about you and your book(s). Always keep the tone of the content friendly but professional. And be sure to include an up-to-date author photo and book cover image where applicable.

Due to Facebook's algorithm, you'll only continue to show up in your followers' newsfeeds if they are commenting or liking your posts on a regular basis; so, you want to keep things interesting and dynamic with regular posts. You can explore Facebook for all kinds of free and/or paid ideas on how to make your page more attractive at another time. For now, here are some specific examples of posts you should be making each and every week, for the next full year, in order to sell more copies of your book:

- **Day One: Promote Your Book's Storefront**

  The first thing you should do is take advantage of the "Shop Now" button on the top of your Facebook page. This is a relatively new Facebook feature—a strong call to action that is located front and centre on top of your page's cover photo—that allows you to link your page directly to the storefront where people can buy your book. Use it!

  Second, at least once per week, you should also post a link to your storefront that will go out as a reminder to your page followers' newsfeeds. Once in a while, you can also publicly share that link on your personal profile so it goes out to those followers, too. Make sure you display a cover photo of your book along with that link. In general, posts with photos tend to garner more attention.

- **Days Two and Three: Share Your Blog Posts**

  Your goal is to write and post at least two unique 500-word blog entries per week, every week for the next year. It's because this is exactly the type of variety and diversity in content that will keep your followers engaged and continually clicking on your links.

- **Day Four: Cross Promote Your Other Social Media Sites**

  Once per week, post a link to one of your other social media sites such as Twitter, LinkedIn, or YouTube. Vary the site and the wording you attach to the promotion of that site in your post so that it always appears to be new content in your followers' newsfeeds each week.

- ## Day Five: Promote Your Contest

In the chapter about blogging, we talked about how contests can add that extra little incentive to buyers who may be on the fence about choosing your book over another one on the same topic. Not only can you promote that contest in the form of a blog entry, but you can also promote it by creating an event on your Facebook page (Facebook Help Centre, 2015a). The event creates a fixed deadline for the draw date of that contest, which adds to the excitement and creates a sense of urgency in your followers to buy the book now. Highlight that contest once weekly.

- ## Day Six: Post a "Joke of the Week" or a "Saying of the Week"

Keep things lighthearted and entertaining by either posting a joke or an inspirational quote of some kind related to your book's topic once per week. Call it your "joke of the week" or "saying of the week" to keep your readers anticipating the next one that will come along next week. You can quickly find all kinds of jokes and inspirational quotes in simple Google searches. Be sure to credit the author you are quoting when you do this, though, just as you would want others to quote you as the source if they posted a phrase from your copyrighted book. Always respect other artists' copyright.

- ## Day Seven: Post a Favourable Review of Your Book or Your Bestseller Status

If you only have one or two favourable reviews to work with in the beginning, not to worry. You can quote different portions of these reviews each week to change things up a bit. If or when your book is publicly listed as a bestseller anywhere, you'll definitely want to post that, too! People will respect and read books that are publicly endorsed by other readers as long as those endorsements are from legitimate sources that can be substantiated by public links.

You'll find this is a really good start to self-promotion on Facebook because it's quick and simple while still providing the variety of content that will keep your followers interested. Some days it will only take you five minutes to post your content; but even on those days when you're trying to find content (such as jokes or quotes) on Google to post to your page, you'll see you can still easily do it in less than 20 minutes per social media site.

You can accomplish a lot in only six hours per week when you're devoting four of those hours to writing two solid blog posts and using the other two hours to post a variety of relevant content on social media. If you do this on a consistent basis with a very specific goal in mind, you'll definitely start to sell more books and make progress toward your goal. You'll see. Then next year will be easier. When you set next year's goal to continue building on your success, you'll be several steps ahead in terms of reusable content, motivation to create new content, and know-how about how to bring it altogether profitably.

REDIRECT TRAFFIC TO YOUR STOREFRONT USING TWITTER

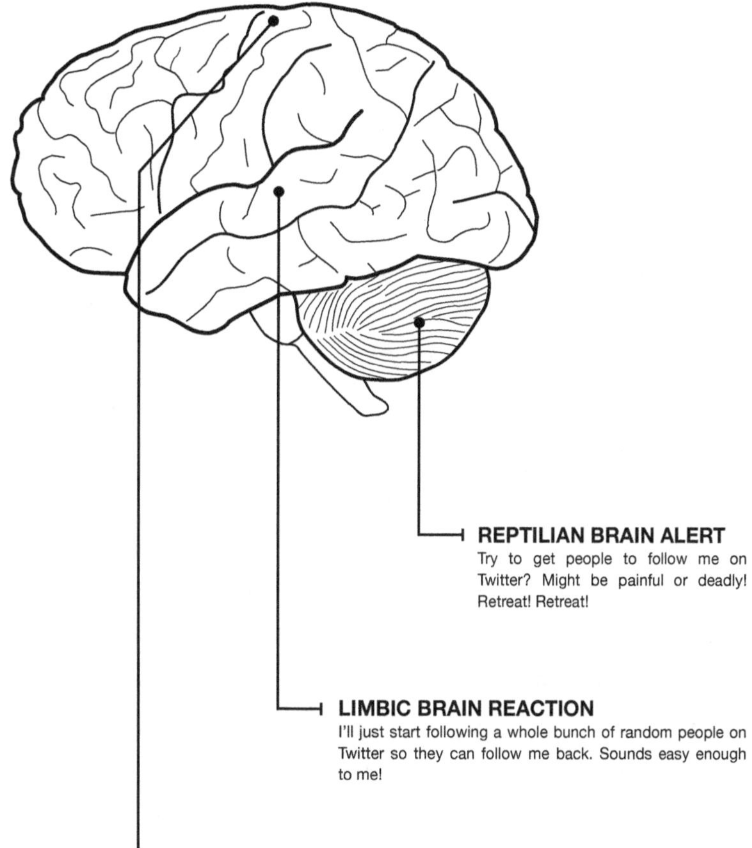

Consider Twitter the abridged version of Facebook. It is a great place to post brief comments or links to your storefront, blog entries, and other relevant online content. Whereas your posts on Facebook can be as long as you want, you are limited to 140 characters per post (known as a "tweet") on Twitter. This is all the rage in online marketing these days. Everyone is tweeting, and that's why you should be, too! Never before has it been easier to reach a global audience so quickly—not to mention free of charge. Your only investment is your time (unless you have someone else tweeting for you, of course).

The whole idea behind Twitter is to utilize the power of word-of-mouth advertising by getting as many people to follow you as possible, and you start this process by beginning to follow others first. From there, you can begin to build on your audience by posting relevant content that your followers will, hopefully, "retweet" (RT) to their followers. If the content in the RT is interesting enough to this additional audience, it may well cause them to begin following you, too.

Another way to gain followers and attract interest from people outside of your current list of followers is by including hashtags in each of your tweets. A hashtag is to Twitter what a keyword is to blogging. For example, the keyword "How to Sell a Book" could be formatted into a hashtag that looks like this: #HowToSellABook. When you include a hashtag like this as part of your tweet, it will show up in all searches performed for that phrase on Twitter. It might entice even more people to view your profile and eventually begin to follow you, too.

Mentions are another way to reach a larger audience. For example, to create a link to Kim Staflund's profile within your tweet, you would include the mention @kimstaflund inside the text. Doing this will share that user's Twitter profile with your followers which may lead them to RT your tweet back to theirs. I do this for all the companies who review my books and any of the online publications I receive additional publicity in. Mentioning them on my profile not only gives me and my books more credibility in the eyes of my followers, it is also my way of saying thank you to them for the review/publicity by introducing them to an extended audience.

As with Facebook, you need to be sure your tweets about yourself and your book are not only promotional, but also helpful and interesting to your followers. Try to imagine what you would like to read if you were viewing your tweets. Not all of them have to mention your book. Another thing you want to do is ensure your daily content is slightly different on Twitter than it is on Facebook so that your followers on both sites will stay engaged and interested in both. For example:

- **Day One: Promote Your Contest**

  You can alternate your tweets to redirect people to your blog entry about the contest one week and your Facebook event page the next week, for the sake of variety. Two popular hashtags on Twitter are #contest and #win. Be sure to include those in each tweet about your contest as often as you can.

- **Day Two: Cross Promote Your Other Social Media Sites**

  Once per week, post a link to one of your other social media sites such as Facebook, LinkedIn, or YouTube. Vary the site and the wording you attach to the promotion of that site in your post so that it always appears to be new content in your followers' newsfeeds each week.

- **Day Three: Post a "Joke of the Week" or a "Saying of the Week"**

  Some of the more popular hashtags on Twitter include #funny, #jokes, and #funnyjokes. You can use these to attract attention to this weekly post; however, it doesn't leave much room in your 140 character tweet for an actual joke and a punchline, does it? You'll either have to keep your jokes and/or inspirational quotes pretty short, or you can use this day as an opportunity to search for someone else's tweet of a funny joke or inspirational quote and RT it to your followers. You may just get an appreciative new follower by doing so, and that new follower may one day buy your book.

- ## Day Four: Promote Your Book's Storefront

Once per week, you should tweet a link to your book's storefront that will go out as a reminder to your Twitter followers in their newsfeeds. Be sure to upload a picture of your book's cover as part of this tweet if you haven't already uploaded it as the background image for your Twitter page.

- ## Days Five and Six: Share Your Blog Posts

If you're ambitious enough the first week, how about writing two extra blog entries so you can post different content on Twitter than you've posted on Facebook earlier in the week? It's not necessary, but it's a great way to improve the variety of your advertising across all these sites. At the very least, make sure you always post your blog entries on different days. Keep it interesting and varied that way.

- ## Day Seven: Post a Favourable Review of Your Book or Your Bestseller Status

Make sure to tweet links to favourable book reviews and any other publicity you receive for yourself and your book at least once per week. You can also mention the publication as part of the tweet (i.e., @TheBookbag) to give you and your book more credibility in the eyes of your followers while also thanking that organization by introducing them to your followers.

Do these things on a regular basis on Twitter, and the next thing you know, you'll have hundreds of Twitter followers who are subscribed to receive your tweets on a regular basis. The more relevant, interesting, and consistent your tweets are, the greater your top-of-mind awareness becomes among potential new customers just as it is with traditional advertising.

You can visit the Polished Publishing Group Twitter page @PPG-Publishing and my personal Twitter page @KimStaflund for more ideas and inspiration on the types of tweets you might want to create to promote yourself and your book. There are a wide variety of topic matter and content examples to choose from there.

REDIRECT TRAFFIC TO YOUR STOREFRONT USING LINKEDIN

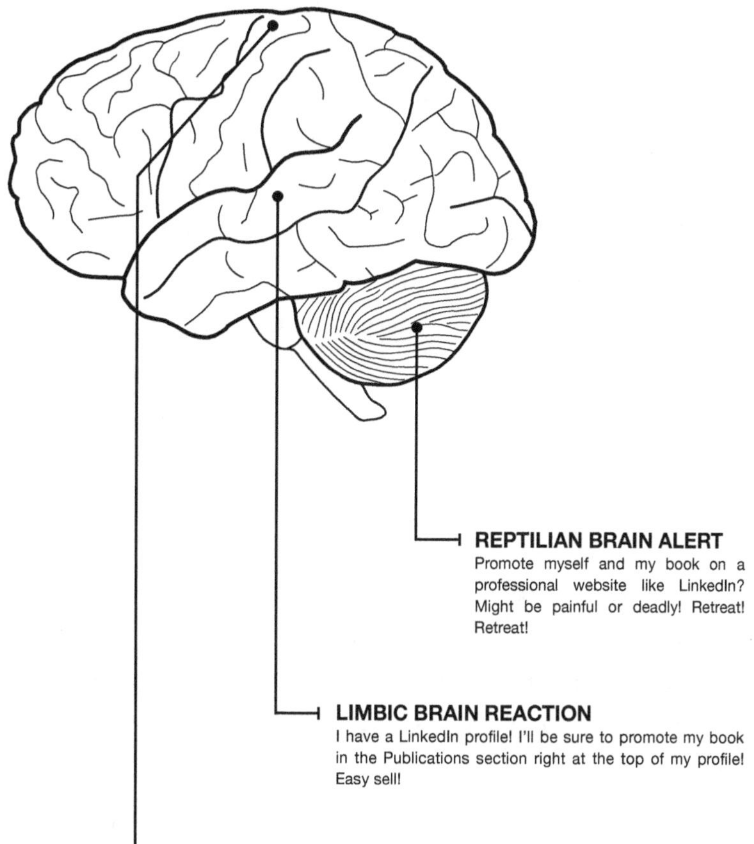

Think of LinkedIn as Facebook for business professionals. As the largest business networking site in the world, and the second-largest social networking site overall (after Facebook), LinkedIn acts as your online resume where you can highlight your expertise within your field. You should definitely feature your published book on your profile so that anyone who views your profile will see it. There is a section of the profile called Publications that will link directly to your book's storefront that you can display right at the top of your profile.

If your primary purpose for using LinkedIn is to promote your book, then be sure your entire profile establishes you as an authority on your book's topic. That said, if you're also using LinkedIn to network with colleagues at another full-time job, or to find work in a field outside your book's topic matter, then you need to be more subtle about how you're promoting your book. In this case, it's best to keep the Publications section a bit lower down on your profile. The reason is that current and potential employers may view your book in a negative light; they may fear your lack of commitment to your job within their organization if promotion of your book appears to be too "in your face" in your profile.

- ## Days One and Seven: Share Your Blog Posts

    You can post links to your blog entries on your profile page's status updates once in a while, but not so often as to annoy your connections. On LinkedIn, you can join groups that are related to your field; so, perhaps a better way to post and share them is within these groups (LinkedIn, 2015). It's a great way to drive more traffic to your blog entries—traffic in the form of people who have already shown an interest in your topic by virtue of the LinkedIn group you met them in. This may lead to them sending you a connection request and eventually also to buying your book via the Publications section on your profile page.

LinkedIn offers an outstanding opportunity to market your book, but don't push people too hard here (i.e., by sending them unsolicited email requests to buy your book, or things like that). Build your audience gradually by posting relevant and informative blog entries twice a week to groups that are interested in your topic matter, and only occasionally as status updates directly from your profile page. Engage in conversations with those who post comments to your blog entries and status updates. Let your audience get to know you by replying to their posts and answering their questions. Then let the rest of it happen organically. Always be professional on this site.

The best way to understand LinkedIn is to start using it, if you aren't already. Create an account. Then look at these two pages for inspiration on how you might build your own business and personal pages: Polished Publishing Group (PPG) | LinkedIn and Kim Staflund - Canada | LinkedIn.

REDIRECT TRAFFIC TO YOUR STOREFRONT USING YOUTUBE

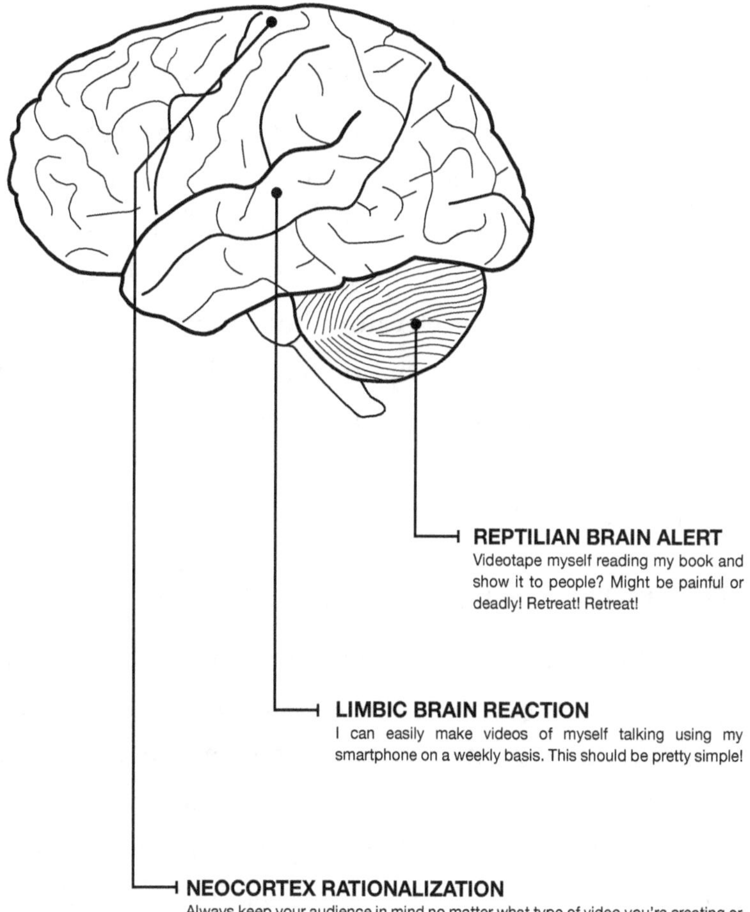

As the second most searched website in the world (after Google), YouTube is a popular social media site on which users can upload, share, and view videos free of charge. This makes it a fantastic tool that authors can use to advertise themselves and their books online.

If you've never made a video of any kind before, not to worry; neither had most of the other authors who are now using YouTube regularly (the author of this book included). Get some practice by starting small at first:

- **Day Four: Camera-shy authors can start with just their voices**

  Take an audio recording (.MP3) of you reciting your book's elevator pitch; then, using a user-friend program like Microsoft Movie Maker, convert it to a YouTube-friendly video file (.MP4) by adding your book's front cover image to the file. Upload it to YouTube and copy the text of your elevator pitch along with a link to your book's storefront into the description box under the video. Also make sure the title, tags, and category sections are complete. This is one of the YouTube links you can share with others via Facebook and Twitter on the designated days.

- **OR on Day Four: Create and Post an Alfresco Video Reading**

  When you feel a little braver, take a video recording (.MP4) of yourself reading a chapter from your book and post that online. You can make it much more interesting by shooting it as a scene outside—by reading from your book with a picturesque display of your own town or city in the background. You can add music to the file, if you choose, in addition to filling out all the standard sections—the title, tags, category, and description—with as many of your popular keywords as you possibly can.

Always keep your audience in mind no matter what type of video you're creating or sharing. It isn't enough to just read from your book; rather, think about what your readers will want to know about you and your book. Your goal is the same here as it is on every other site you're posting content to; it's an opportunity for potential new audience members to get to know you and your book a little better, to build on that top-of-mind awareness we're trying to build on. Just as it is when you're writing blog entries, remember that how-tos, answers to FAQs, expert interviews, insights on characters and their development, and entertaining stories are all popular topic matters that will grab people's attention.

Keep your YouTube videos short. In this "instant soup society" of ours, even YouTube users have short attention spans, so it's better to upload five three-minute videos than it is to upload one 15-minute video whenever possible. More videos that utilize even more of your top keywords will also provide more varied selling opportunities.

In addition to creating my own videos, I always make sure to ask the interviewers of any Skype, radio, or television interviews I've done to send me an .MP3 or .MP4 of our interview session. I upload that to my company YouTube channel along with an introduction to the interviewers and their station in the description box below the video. It's a way to thank them by opening them up to an expanded audience through my channel, and it's also a way for me to attract some of their listeners to me by coupling their top keywords together with mine.

As it is with all the other sites, the best way to learn and understand YouTube is to start using it if you aren't already. Create an account then look at this page for inspiration on the types of videos you can share on there to promote yourself and your book: www.youtube.com/user/PolishedPublishing.

REDIRECT TRAFFIC TO YOUR STOREFRONT USING PAY-PER-CLICK (PPC) ADVERTISING

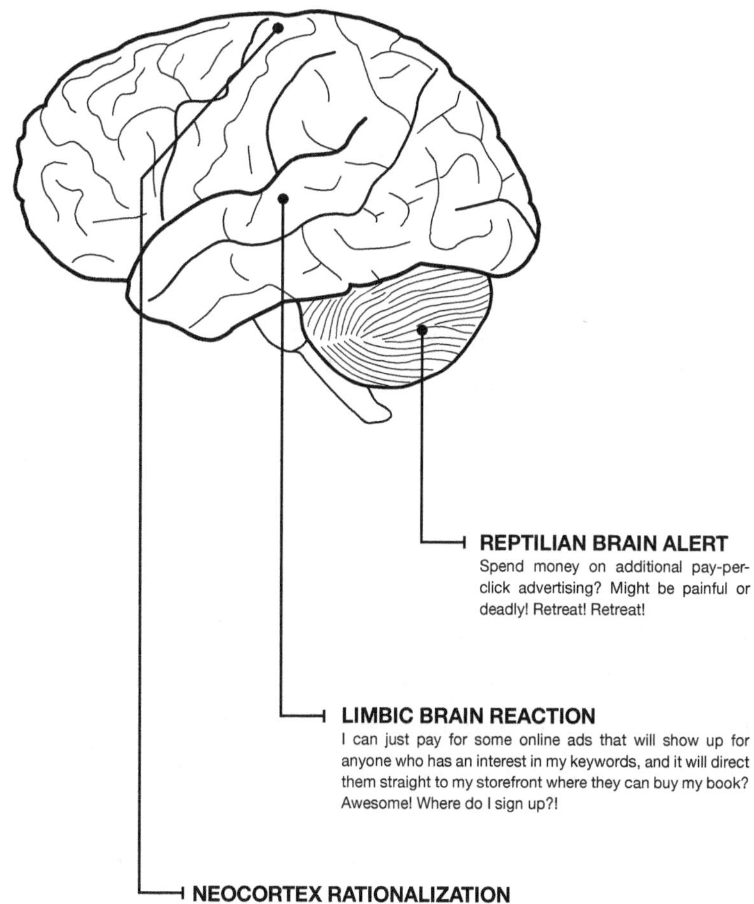

We've looked at many of the free online advertising options available to authors on a few of the top social media sites. Now, let's look at a popular paid option that takes the power of keywords to a whole other level: pay-per-click advertising (Wikipedia, 2015e). For anyone wishing to supercharge their *gratis* social media advertising, they might wish to complement their blogging with a targeted PPC campaign:

Pay-per-click (PPC), also called cost-per-click, is an internet advertising model used to direct traffic to websites, in which advertisers pay the publisher (typically a website owner) when the ad is clicked. It is defined simply as "the amount spent to get an advertisement clicked." The cost of a PPC campaign depends on a few different factors:

1. Where is it being run (i.e., Google, Yahoo, Bing, Facebook, or LinkedIn)?

2. What region is it being targeted to (i.e., one city, province, or state, the entire country, the entire continent)?

3. How long does the campaign run for (i.e., for a specified amount of time, or until a specified advertising budget has been used up)?

Google, Yahoo, and Bing PPC campaigns are designed to target specific keywords that users might type into the search engine. (Two example keywords that PPG has used in the past are "How to Publish a Book" and "How to Sell a Book.") Facebook campaigns are designed to target a specific Facebook demographic such as "female users, age 20–40" or "all users" who have expressed an interest in "book publishing," for example. LinkedIn offers a great audience for non-fiction books—especially those related to business, including sales and marketing.

When you start a PPC campaign, you agree to pay X dollars per each click on your ads that are redirected to your specified landing site (hence the term "pay-per-click"). The landing site can be your own website, an online article or blog you've written, a YouTube video you've posted, your storefront on Kobo or iTunes where your book is currently for sale, or wherever else you want to direct traffic to at that moment. But keep this in mind: the landing site is as crucial to your success as the PPC ad itself is. The ad needs to contain an enticing enough message to make people want to click on it, and the landing site to which they are redirected should contain a strong call to action that allows them to buy your product or service right then and there. That's the key! Ask for the sale and there's a good chance you'll get it! With that in mind, I highly recommend you direct the majority—if not *all*—of your PPC-driven traffic right to your storefront. You want people to be able to click and buy, click and buy, click and buy as easily as possible.

• Days One through Seven: PPC advertising

If you decide to add paid PPC advertising to your campaign this year, run it daily. And *watch* it daily—that's the key. "Set it and forget it" is a non-existent term when it comes to PPC campaigns. You need to review your campaigns every single day to ensure you're getting the most value for your investment. If you're seeing very few clicks, or not enough of your clicks are turning into sales, then you need to test and tweak the keywords you're using to attract the type of traffic and response that you want.

Online publications (e.g., EzineArticles.com) use the power of PPC advertising to drive more traffic to their websites, but they take it a step further. They have arranged partnerships with various search engines to display their PPC ads on the articles within their publications that have matching keywords. The search engine pays the online publication a portion of the PPC proceeds for any of the clicks that come directly from their articles; and they, in turn, share a small portion of those proceeds with the authors of the articles. This is another great reason for authors to do some of their blogging in the form of online advertorials. It's an opportunity to earn incremental income while promoting your products and services and directing more traffic to your site.

To gain a better understanding of how PPC works and how much it costs, contact the websites mentioned earlier. Ask them about their own pricing structures and policies. Each of them is a little different.

BOOK PUBLICISTS (ADVERTISING VERSUS PUBLICITY)

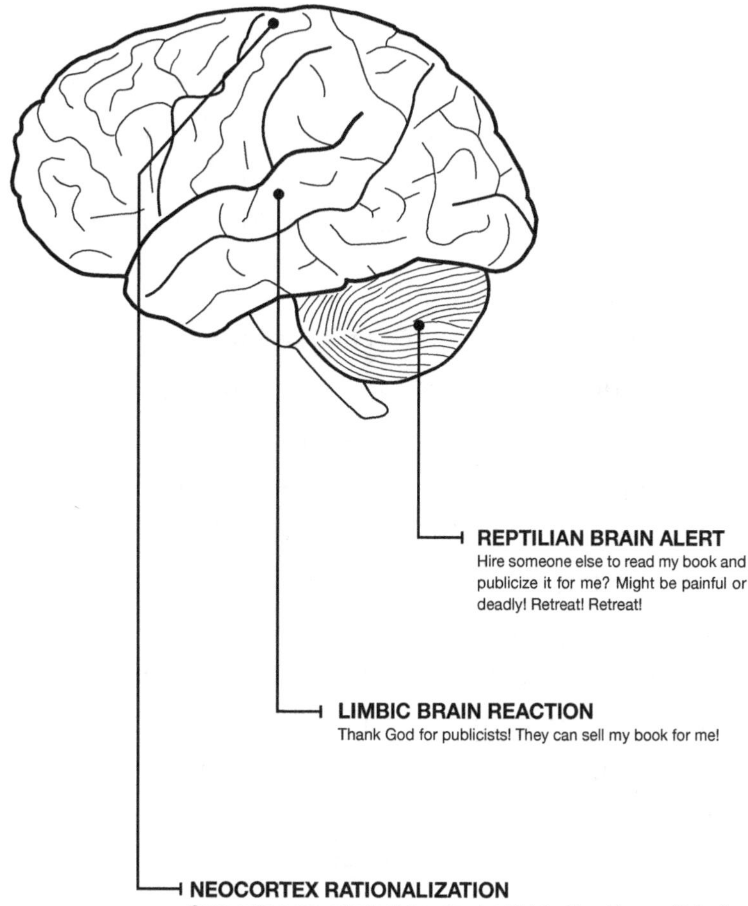

Up to this point, we've discussed ways you can market and sell your book using various forms of both free and paid online *advertising*. Now we're going to talk about *publicity*. In her ebook titled *The Power of Publicity for Your Book,* Marsha Friedman (2014) provides us with a clear distinction between the two:

> By definition, publicity is not advertising; it's coverage by the media of people, events and issues deemed to be of interest to their audiences.
>
> . . . The nice thing about publicity, also referred to as "earned media," is that you don't buy it; you earn it. If you can get a journalist or talk show host interested in your story idea or topic, you might be interviewed for an article, asked to write an article for publication, or invited to be interviewed as a guest on a radio or TV show.
>
> The endorsement of traditional media, even if it's simply mentioning your name, has always been marketing gold to anyone trying to build a reputation as an author and gain visibility for their book. (p. 6)

Some authors misunderstand the role of publicists. They hire a publicity firm assuming that organization will advertise and sell their book(s) for them, but this is incorrect. The true role of a publicist is to garner publicity for their *client*—to get that author mentioned in the media via Associated Press-style articles and press releases written about the topic(s) in his or her book, and by promoting that author as an industry expert in his or her field. The idea is to attract newspaper, radio, and television interviews that will highlight the publicist's client within the mainstream media. The by-product of this publicity is a heightened interest in the author, which should boost sales of his or her book much like advertising does.

Both advertising and publicity are about putting yourself in front of a larger audience as often as possible to build on (and maintain) that top-of-mind awareness we talked about earlier; but, by contrast, advertising is essentially *you* talking about yourself and your book whereas publicity is the *media* talking about you and your book. Obviously, when someone else is talking about you, it has more credibility in the eyes of the public. That's the power of publicity.

It is possible to generate publicity on your own, free of charge, without hiring a publicist to write the news stories for you. Marsha (Friedman, 2014) offers some helpful tips about this in her ebook, as well:

> You can hire PR professionals to help you get publicity, but you can also work at getting it for yourself. . . . for a newspaper, you might write a short, bona fide news story, or a list of tips that address a problem relevant to your book. For TV and radio, briefly describe the topic you can address and what you will contribute. . . . Most mass media are focused on issues and events in the news today, so you're much more likely to get publicity if you can speak to something going on now. That's not as difficult as it sounds, but it does require creative thinking. (p. 6)

There is a definite benefit to hiring a publicist to do all this for you, though. Publicity firms have developed long-standing relationships with all the "movers and shakers" in the media, and their staff knows exactly how to format news stories to have an "Associated Press" appeal that is more likely to be picked up. They watch the news regularly, so they're aware of what is going on and how to tie you and your book topics into current events. Hiring a publicist is somewhat expensive but, in my opinion, it's worth the investment when you're working with a reputable firm.

How expensive is it? Well, it depends. There are different types of publicists out there. Some firms want a retainer, much like a law firm, and they will charge their clients for time spent researching, writing, and contacting the media as well as for telephone charges, postage fees, and any other materials they create for you (i.e., printing and copying). And then there are the firms that use a pay-for-performance business model where they charge only one lump sum fee in the beginning and guarantee a certain amount of publicity along with that lump sum fee.

So, again, to clarify: If you want someone to publish your book and provide you with worldwide distribution channels to sell it through, hire a publisher; if you want someone to sell your book for you, hire a salesperson; if you want someone to advertise and market your book for you, hire an ad agency; and if you want publicity for yourself and your book, hire a publicist. Or, you can manage your own publishing, distribution, sales, advertising, marketing, and publicity by yourself using all of the techniques discussed in this book and my two previous books.

As with everything, there are pros and cons to hiring any of these professionals. It's important to do your homework to determine which one is best for you or whether you even want to hire one at all. You may decide to do it all on your own. Just make sure you're doing *something*. Remember, you'll sell many more books if you're in the driver's seat than you will if you leave it all up to your publisher. Anytime you find yourself questioning that, just think *Jack Canfield!* Then soldier ahead!

Good luck, my introverted friends. From the bottom of my heart, I wish you much success with the sale of your books. I hope you sell many copies, earn a healthy profit, and maybe even become a bestseller in the process. I hope you achieve your goal, whatever it is. That is my wish for you.

"I saw myself as a businessman first. Too many actors, writers, and artists think that marketing is beneath them. But no matter what you do in life, selling is part of it."

~Arnold Schwarzenegger, quote from his autobiography
Total Recall: My Unbelievably True Life Story (2012)

BIBLIOGRAPHY

ACX. (2015). *Frequently Asked Questions: Royalties and Earnings.* Retrieved May 9, 2015, from ACX: an Amazon Platform : https://www.acx.com/help/royalties-and-earnings/201689000. (Accessed May 9, 2015)

Blakely, S. (2011). "Sara Blakely of Spanx Speaks at The Edge Connection—Atlanta, GA." Retrieved May 2, 2015, from *Official Spanx, Inc.* Channel: https://www.youtube.com/watch?v=m1tTZSuHJKM

Byrne, R. (2006). The Secret. Retrieved May 2, 2015, from https://docs.google.com/file/d/0ByqvewEmgwYXZkxXSEM0bENvWjQ/edit?pli=1

Cameron, J. (2002). *The Artist's Way.* Retrieved May 2, 2015, from Google Books: https://books.google.ca/books?id=ZaC7Br7sMBMC&pg=PT146&lpg=PT146&dq=Do+not+call+procrastination+laziness.+Call+it+fear.&source=bl&ots=Y4SCJfgVtR&sig=DJ0wZGcs1UpUXbWc7xs7-UUuheL8&hl=en&sa=X&ei=xe4WVZLfKcvboASJnYHYCA&ved=0CC0Q6AEwBA#v=onepage&q=Do%20not%20ca

CreateSpace. (2015). *Understanding Royalties.* Retrieved May 9, 2015 from CreateSpace: https://www.createspace.com/Products/Book/Royalties.jsp (Accessed May 9, 2015)

Dubuc, B. (2015). "The Evolutionary Layers of the Human Brain" *The Brain from Top to Bottom.* Retrieved May 2, 2015, from thebrain.mcgill.ca: http://thebrain.mcgill.ca/flash/d/d_05/d_05_cr/d_05_cr_her/d_05_cr_her.html

EzineArticles. (2015, June 6). "Expert Authors, Kim Staflund." Retrieved June 6, 2015, from EzineArticles: http://ezinearticles.com/?expert=Kim_Staflund

Facebook Help Centre. (2015a). *Creating & Editing Events.* Retrieved June 27, 2015, from Facebook Help Centre: https://www.facebook.com/help/131325477007622/

Facebook Help Centre. (2015b). *Should I create a Page or allow people to follow my public updates from my personal account?* Retrieved June 27, 2015, from Facebook Help Centre: https://www.facebook.com/help/203141666415461

Free Dictionary, The. (2015a). *Advertising Selling Marketing.* Retrieved June 6, 2015, from The Free Dictionary by Farlex: http://www.thefreedictionary.com/

Free Dictionary, The. (2015b). *Elevator Pitch.* Retrieved June 20, 2015, from The Free Dictionary by Farlex.com: http://encyclopedia.thefreedictionary.com/elevator+pitch

Friedman, M. (2014). *The Power of Publicity for Your Book.* Retrieved June 6, 2015, from emsincorporated.com: http://emsincorporated.com/wp-content/uploads/2014/03/Power-of-Publicity-for-Your-Book.pdf

GoDaddy. (2015). *Online Stores.* Retrieved June 21, 2015, from GoDaddy.com: https://ca.godaddy.com/ecommerce/online-store.aspx

Kobo. (2015). *Writing Life User Guide.* Retrieved May 9, 2015, from Kobobooks.com: http://download.kobobooks.com/writinglife/en-US/KWL-User-Guide.pdf)

Kruse, K. (2015). *Zig Ziglar: 10 Quotes That Can Change Your Life.* Retrieved May 2, 2015, from Forbes.com: http://www.forbes.com/sites/kevinkruse/2012/11/28/zig-ziglar-10-quotes-that-can-change-your-life/

LinkedIn. (2015). *Groups - Getting Started.* Retrieved June 27, 2015, from LinkedIn: https://help.linkedin.com/app/answers/detail/a_id/1164/~/groups---getting-started

PayPal. (2015, June 21). About Us. Retrieved June 21, 2015, from Paypal: https://www.paypal-media.com/ca/about

Polished Publishing Group (2015a). *Polished Publishing Group Facebook Page*. Retrieved May 2, 2015, from Polished Publishing Group (PPG): https://www.facebook.com/245465516591/photos/a.10150415163541592.353270.245465516591/10152326991021592/?type=3&theater

Polished Publishing Group (2015b). *PPG Publishing Agreement and Production Questionnaire.* Retrieved May 9, 2015, from Polished Publishing Group (PPG): http://www.polishedpublishinggroup.com/Publishing_Agreement_JHB6.html

Schwarzenegger, A. (2012). Total Recall: My Unbelievably True Life Story. New York, NY: Simon & Schuster Paperbacks.

Staflund, K. (2013). *How to Publish a Book in Canada . . . and Sell Enough Copies to Make a Profit!* Calgary, Alberta: Polished Publishing Group.

Staflund, K. (2014) *How to Publish a Bestselling Book . . . and Sell it WORLDWIDE Based on Value, Not Price!* Calgary, Alberta: Polished Publishing Group.

Urban Dictionary. (2007). *What's In It for Me? WIIFM.* Retrieved from UrbanDictionary.com: http://www.urbandictionary.com/define.php?term=WIIFM (Accessed May 17, 2015)

Wikipedia (2015a). *Digital Rights Management.* Retrieved July 13, 2015) from Wikipedia, The Free Encyclopedia: https://en.wikipedia.org/wiki/Digital_rights_management.

Wikipedia. (2015b). *.EPUB ebooks.* Retrieved June 6, 2015, from Wikipedia, The Free Encyclopedia: https://en.wikipedia.org/wiki/EPUB

Wikipedia. (2015c). *Everyday Low Price pricing strategy.* Retrieved May 17, 2015, from Wikipedia, The Free Encyclopedia: http://en.wikipedia.org/wiki/Everyday_low_price.

Wikipedia (2015d). *Fifty Shades of Grey – E L James.* Retrieved May 2, 2015, from Wikipedia The Free Encyclopedia: http://en.wikipedia.org/wiki/Fifty_Shades_of_Grey

Wikipedia (2015e) *Pay per Click.* Retrieved June 28, 2015, from Wikipedia, The Free Encyclopedia: http://en.wikipedia.org/wiki/Pay_per_click

Wikipedia (2015f). *Print on Demand.* Retrieved May 2, 2015, from Wikipedia, The Free Encyclopedia: http://en.wikipedia.org/wiki/Print_on_demand

Wikipedia (2015g). *Search engine optimization.* Retrieved June 24, 2015, from Wikipedia, The Free Encyclopedia: https://en.wikipedia.org/wiki/Search_engine_optimization

Wikipedia. (2015h, May 17). *Top of mind awareness.* Retrieved from Wikipedia, The Free Encyclopedia: http://en.wikipedia.org/wiki/Top-of-mind_awareness

Wikipedia. (2015i, May 17). *Value-based pricing.* Retrieved May 17, 2015, from Wikipedia, The Free Encyclopedia: http://en.wikipedia.org/wiki/Value-based_pricing

INDEX

ABOUT THE AUTHOR

As the founder and publisher at Polished Publishing Group (PPG), Kim Staflund works with businesses and individuals around the world to produce truly professional-quality audiobooks, ebooks, paperbacks, and hardcovers using the supported self-publishing business model. As a bestselling author and sales coach, she shows them how to sell their books using all the effective traditional and online tricks of the trade.

Think of PPG as a skilled project manager and sales coach for authors. Supported self-publishing is intended for serious-minded authors with an entrepreneurial mindset who wish to earn a profit from the commercial sale of their books, and who would rather hire a professional project manager with industry expertise to help them publish, sell, and distribute their books worldwide, rather than spend copious hours awkwardly managing the project themselves.

In addition to her book publishing background, Kim has a substantial sales and sales management history that includes new business development, both inside and outside account management of all types and sizes of companies, and personnel management and leadership experience within unionized and non-unionized environments. Add her firsthand knowledge of records management, process management, and project management into the mix, and you have everything that is required in a professional book publisher to help authors succeed.

Kim's number one priority in each of these roles has always been, and will always be, to earn (and keep) the trust of each of her clients by providing ethical and thoughtful customer service that meets or exceeds their expectations.

Kim's intention in writing this book is to help introverted authors soar to new heights and enjoy more success in the sale of their books. Happy selling and good luck to you all!

BOOK REVIEWS

How to Publish a Book in Canada
. . . and Sell Enough Copies to Make a Profit!

Ebook ISBN: 978-0-9864869-7-5
Paperback ISBN: 978-0-9864869-6-8

"Staflund's stated goal is to give Canadian authors insight into what it takes to produce a salable book in Canada, get it into the hands of the desired demographic, and earn a healthy profit in the process. In this, she has succeeded admirably."

~ForeWord Reviews, Clarion Review

"A good source for writers of all experience levels seeking to publish quality books in Canada."

~Kirkus Reviews

"This book is a real, and I mean real, learning tool . . . You will know how to do what the title states when you finish Kim Staflund's book."

~Palmetto Review

"*How to Publish a Book in Canada* is a very instructive book for any author—in and out of Canada. Though the book is specifically for Canadian authors, writers from any country will gain insight from this book."

~Pacific Book Review

"Staflund's personal stories, humor, and examples throughout makes this book entertaining as well as instructional . . . *How to Publish a Book in Canada* is a great investment for future publishers—both in Canada and outside of Canada."

~Penn Book Review

How to Publish a Bestselling Book
. . . and Sell It Worldwide Based on Value, Not Price!

Ebook ISBN: 978-0-9864869-9-9
Paperback ISBN: 978-0-9864869-8-2

"'How to Publish a Bestselling Book' is exceptional, practical, detailed, comprehensive, and thoroughly 'user friendly' from beginning to end. If you are an aspiring writer seeking commercial success as a published author, then you need a copy of Kim Staflund's 'How to Publish a Bestselling Book.'"

~Midwest Book Review

". . . Staflund gives good advice and it's remarkably far-reaching, considering that it covers several countries . . . [A]n enlightening, helpful book which gives you an excellent introduction to the business of publishing."

~The Bookbag

"As a veteran of the publishing industry, Staflund certainly is an authoritative voice and provides helpful guidance in her newest book, *How to Publish a Bestselling Book* . . . [A] must-read for any writer hoping to publish their next book."

~Hollywood Book Reviews

"Staflund's respect for the writers at the heart of the publishing process makes this a worthwhile addition to any aspiring author's bookshelf."

~ForeWord Reviews, Clarion Review

"[T]here is a wealth of information within these pages. . . . Staflund holds nothing back, and because of that, *How to Publish a Bestselling Book* has the feel of a roadmap. Just follow it, and it will easily take you where you want to go."

~Pacific Book Review

CUSTOMIZED SALES COACHING FOR AUTHORS

Want more help? Polished Publishing Group (PPG) is here for you:

FULL-DAY SALES & MARKETING COACHING SESSION FOR AUTHORS

What if, for one full day, you could have a team of people around you who are focused on creating a customized advertising, sales, and marketing strategy specific to your book?*

What if you had a bestselling author, book publisher, and professional sales coach at your disposal facilitating that full-day session?

And what if you could take home a copy of one of these bestselling books (your choice of title), at no extra charge, to keep as a handy reference guide after the session is over?

"Staflund's respect for the writers at the heart of the publishing process makes this a worthwhile edition to any aspiring author's bookshelf."
~ForeWord Reviews, Clarion Review

"A good source for writers of all experience levels seeking to publish quality books in Canada."
~Kirkus Reviews

Bring your fiction or non-fiction audiobook, ebook, paperback, or hardcover with you.
Bring your laptop with its power supply, and bring your desire to succeed.
We've got the rest covered—including internet, lunch, and snacks!
(Session Time: 9 AM to 4 PM)

If you're serious about marketing and selling your book commercially, this information session is perfect for you!

Contact us at www.polishedpublishinggroup.com for more details today.
You'll be glad you did.

*Maximum 12 people per session to ensure a more intimate and informal learning environment for everyone.

Main Website:
www.polishedpublishinggroup.com

PPG Publisher's Blog:
blog.polishedpublishinggroup.com

PPG Writers Forum:
writersforum.polishedpublishinggroup.com

PPG Online Store:
shop.polishedpublishinggroup.com

Facebook:
www.facebook.com/pages/Polished-Publishing-Group.../245465516591

Twitter:
www.twitter.com/ppgpublishing | www.twitter.com/kimstaflund

LinkedIn:
www.linkedin.com/company/polished-publishing-group-ppg-

YouTube:
www.youtube.com/user/PolishedPublishing

EzineArticles:
EzineArticles.com/?expert=Kim_Staflund